On Being Insane

Elliot Gavin Keenan

On Being Insane
Copyright © 2017 by Elliot Gavin Keenan

Cover Design:
Macario Hernandez
Artwork:
Elliot Gavin Keenan
Formatting:
Niki Browning
Editor-in-Chief:
Kristi King-Morgan
Editors:
Valerie Carroll
Connor McDonald

All rights reserved. This book or any portion thereof may not be reproduced or used in any manner whatsoever without the express written permission of the publisher except for the use of brief quotations in a book review.

Printed in the United States of America

First Printing, 2017

ISBN-13: 978-1-947381-02-5
ISBN-10: 1-947381-02-4

Dreaming Big Publications

www.dreamingbigpublications.com

Contents

Dedication	1
Introduction	2
The Little Professor	7
Insane Places	14
Non Sequitur	21
Liminal Spaces	27
Hilton Chicago	33
Three Desks to the Right	39
Autism Diagnostic Observational Assessment	49
Art College	57
RECODE (you = friend)	61
Mattituck 205	67
Cognitive Tunnel Vision	75
International Meeting for Autism Research	85
A Parade of Ghosts	91
Afterword	93
Appendix A. *Reputable Sources for More Information*	97
About the Author	99

Dedication

To Dr. Pinball:
Thank you for teaching me.

To JS:
And I don't know,
don't know,
if we belong together or apart,
except that my soul lingers over the skin of you
— Anne Sexton, *Waking Alone*

Introduction
By: Matthew D. Lerner, PhD

There exist several species of book in the "mental health memoir" genre. The first and arguably most popular is the one offering the author's subjective experience of struggles and successes. Such manuscripts range in tone from journalistic to poetic, offering an intimate, probing portrait of the author as a wellspring of empathy and individual truth; when they touch the reader, they ring like a bell, revealing resonances previously unknown.

A second is the empirical or historical review. Such explorations are often precisely that – a journey into caverns and stacks of psychiatry and psychology's often-tangled attempts to define human experience into neat categories; the inevitable unraveling of first principles of the mind; and, finally, an accounting of the more humble, tenuous attempts of current scientists to make sense of what (little) is known today, and to square that with the life that led the author to embark on such a quest. These are often historically-grounded and -informed, consistent with contemporary literature, and serve as a means to smuggle current clinical science into the hands of readers who might not read peer-reviewed journals.

A third is the clinical perspective. These curious tomes serve as a kind of meta-perspective-taking game in which a searchlight bounces purposefully between the minds of individuals seeking treatment for the challenges they experience, the clinicians who aim to help, and – finally – to the author again, who orients the spinning moral lodestone of the narrative. Such evaluations are notably measured in their approach, both revealing and systematizing, providing both reader and characters new personal insights.

The book you hold in your hand, then, is perhaps something unique to date: a true hybrid representing a potentially new emanation of the genus. Mr. Keenan's abundant literary talents are in bloom here, as he paints hazy boundaries between time and mind, memory and metaphor, emotion and experience. His unflinching willingness to invite the reader into even the most challenging of his experiences provides the floral archway to draw the reader to his side, whispering songs he hopes they might remember. Yet, he situates his feet firmly in the soil of science, allowing his rapid immersion into the world of research to be in equal measure bewildering, illuminating, orienting, and, ultimately heartening; there are real and substantive nuggets of knowledge to be learned from this book (a successful smuggling indeed)! Finally, like a confident jazz improviser, Mr. Keenan does not fear showing his work as he attempts to unearth the coherence and, perhaps, the meaning in each of the relationships he encounters. One cannot help but wonder while reading this book whether, in flickering moments, Mr. Keenan has trained his gaze (quizzically, patiently, cautiously) back on you.

Thus, this is a book that can give an intimate picture and a deep history; it is a fountain of new scientific insights for a lay audience, and revelations for some. Most importantly, perhaps, it may offer a ray of hope – a beacon for those seeking understanding and clarity and a sense of belonging in the world. Not that Mr. Keenan makes this sound easy –instead, he shows both how hard this can be, and how valuable such a sense can be - precisely because it is so ephemeral.

> "But I don't want to go among mad people," Alice remarked.
> "Oh, you can't help that," said the Cat: "we're all mad here. I'm mad. You're mad."
> "How do you know I'm mad?" said Alice.
> "You must be," said the Cat, "or you wouldn't have come here."
> — Lewis Carroll, *Alice in Wonderland*

The house is silent save for a subtle creaking of the floorboards as I sneak through the living room. My parents and my little brother are asleep. Only my three cats are awake; they are following me around the empty house, nudging my ankles with wet, pink noses. They are lonely because my parents are asleep, but I think for a moment that they are asking me not to go. I'm not going to cry yet. One by one, I pick them up and give them each a long hug goodbye, cradling their warm furry bodies in my arms, telling them that I love them very much. Then I pull on my coat and step out through the back door of my parents' house into the bitter cold of a January night.

The exposed bits of my hands and face are red and raw from the chill in the air. But the sky is very clear. I can see the moon and the stars shining. I recognize Orion, and I try to recognize other constellations, but I can't remember any of them.

It feels like a dream. I'm walking along the empty streets of a picturesque suburbia, the setting of my childhood, with old houses and neatly trimmed front lawns. Everything is still. Streetlights dot the way, shining their yellow spotlights onto the pavement.

I head towards the beach first, listening to the rumble of the sea as it creeps up along white sand, the black edges of the waves glinting in the bright moonlight like shards of obsidian. My swing set, a preferred location since my childhood, is gone, so I just stand there for a few moments in quiet contemplation and then head on towards the train tracks.

My phone rings. It's my best friend. I hang up. But it keeps ringing, so I answer.

Suddenly, the screen flashes *temperature warning* and then goes dark. It's too cold for electronics. I stare at it, this now-defunct piece of technology. I don't know why, but tears finally sting my eyes, warming my numb cheeks. It doesn't feel like a dream anymore. Somewhere, not far away, I can hear the approaching train howling into the night. I turn around. It's not my night to die.

The Little Professor

I am born prematurely on December 5, 1995. I spend some time in neonatal, but there are no serious issues; my body is small but functional. I meet all of my major developmental milestones on time. By age three, I can easily read complex words and sentences out loud to my mother. Written words come naturally to me. I love to read books, as I did before I was medicated. By four, I am reading Pokémon chapter books. By six, I am reading J.R.R. Tolkien's *The Hobbit*. Maybe text comes more easily to me than speech. This is known as *hyperlexia* and it's common in kids with autism. I can read almost anything by second grade, but it is hard for me to follow verbal instructions with more than one step.

When I am six years old, my mom brings me to lots of doctors. I don't know why, exactly, but I suspect that it has something to do with the way I am learning penmanship. Many of my letters are backwards. It is impossible to tell the difference between my *P* and my *9*, or my *b* and my *d*. And yet, clearly, I am not dyslexic. The school sends me to get a neuropsychiatric evaluation and my first-grade teacher tells me to try and write backwards on purpose.

Autism. From the Greek *autos*, meaning *self*; literally "self-ism." It was originally described in schizophrenic patients, referring to withdrawn and atypical behavior: being "lost in one's own world." In fact, autism was once considered a type of childhood schizophrenia. But not anymore. The two diagnoses were separated in 1980 with the introduction of *infantile autism* in the DSM-III (Diagnostic and Statistical Manual of Mental Disorders, third edition; the so-called Bible of American psychiatry). In the DSM-IV, *Asperger's disorder* is added to *autistic disorder* along with a few other diagnoses to round out the category of *pervasive developmental disorders*, but in 2013 with the introduction of the DSM-V they are mostly rendered defunct and collected together under *autism spectrum disorder*.

I am seven years old. A man in a white coat (a *developmental neuropsychiatrist*) sits across from me. He asks me to list all the animals I can think of. Naturally, I begin to sort them, first by geographical region starting with Africa: *lion, African elephant, Asian elephant* (I don't want to forget that there are two kinds of elephants)*, hyena, hippopotamus*. Then I lose track, and I decide to re-sort by class in the animal kingdom instead, starting with my favorite, amphibians: *red-eyed tree frog, poison dart frog, salamander, newts…* The doctor stops me. Shortly thereafter I am diagnosed with Asperger's.
(In retrospect, I suppose the typical answer for a seven-year-old would be something along the lines of *cat, dog, bird, fish*. It never occurs to me to sort in order of household familiarity. I am running a different operating system in my brain.)

Amphibians are strange creatures. They start life

in water with gills, but they aren't fish. They eventually develop lungs and breathe air as adults. But even when they undergo this metamorphosis and move onto land, they aren't quite like reptiles, either (even if they superficially resemble lizards). The Greek *amphibios,* from which the term amphibian is derived, literally means *both kinds of life.* Amphibians are in-betweens, occupying what seems like a liminal space; maybe this is why I like them so much. You can metamorphose into an air-breathing creature that looks like a lizard, but you'll never really be a lizard. Do amphibians ever long to eschew their newfound lungs and return to their life under the surface of the water?

I begin to undergo my own metamorphosis. When my parents aren't looking, I read the books the doctors advised them to buy, the Tony Attwoods and Oasis Guides; their spines are clean and uncreased. They describe *little professors*, kids with extensive bodies of knowledge in specific areas of interest, who are limited in their social ability. I recognize myself in the books. I am an uncoordinated, isolated child with a host of eccentricities, including an unusually pedantic way of speaking. I don't have many friends, if any at all. I never have friends for long.

I also learn about the DSM, a catalog of mental disorders; I'm drawn to its way of classifying human loneliness in the same way that I might classify interesting frogs. Later that night, I Google search DSM criteria for many different diagnoses. I begin to think that I would like to be a psychologist, too.

When I'm a little kid, I don't care much about other people. But I like to read. I read all kinds of things. My great-grandmother tells my mom that she never sees me without my nose in a book. But I don't often talk for the purpose of conversation; I keep mostly to myself.

Then I learn about Asperger's. Maybe the man in the white coat is the harbinger of this change in me, or maybe I've been coming around to it all along. Once I know what makes me different, I become obsessed with understanding it completely. Memorizing the DSM criteria doesn't feed this newfound hunger, but it is a start; I have to know exactly the boundaries of what qualifies as autistic behavior so that I can cross those boundaries. I want to imitate normalcy. I want other people to like me. What does that make me? An amphibian, not quite aqueous and not quite terrestrial? But once you breathe air, you can't go back to the quiet darkness submerged in liquid. You'll stay there, damp, peering in at the water's murky edge.

In the summer, my grandma takes me to the park. It is the closest thing to wilderness I know of in my short, suburban existence. There is a nature club for kids there, and I am allowed to muck around the bank of the lake and search for frogs and salamanders. I am obsessed with amphibians; I know a lot about them. I rarely find anything good at the park, but I like going there. I love swinging on the swing set. When it starts to get dark, my grandma takes me to get dinner, usually at Friendly's, where I always eat chicken fingers. I mostly like to do the same things and eat the same things over again.

I have had special interests in particular topics (amphibians, Pokémon, psychology) for my whole life. My special interest might have saved someone's life once.

It is a sunny day in late March, and the psychiatric inpatients of 3 North whose behavior has been deemed acceptable enough to go outside are standing in the small green patch of lawn that makes up the courtyard of the hospital, playing catch with a battered football. It is a Saturday. On Saturdays we get to spend half an hour outside, twice a day. Most of us are too heavily medicated to run for long. So we just stand in place and toss the ball back and forth, often missing.

After about fifteen minutes of outside time, my friend (an especially tall and broad young man who got admitted after breaking down a door, which seems easy for someone of his imposing stature) and I sit down on one of the picnic tables. We're chatting about different people at the hospital when he mentions that his jaw is hurting. *Are you alright?* I ask, watching him fiddle with his jaw.

My left jaw is locked up, he says, with some difficulty. *My neck is starting to hurt too.*

I'm quiet for a moment. Processing. Then I ask, *Did they give you any new meds?*

Yeah. Haldol.

I know a possible case of neuroleptic malignant syndrome (a reaction to antipsychotic drugs that is, left untreated, likely to be fatal) when I see it. I run to the nursing staff who are standing by the door. They bring him inside. We are waiting for the nurses, who are waiting for the doctors. (The doctors would, in turn, wait for the ambulance. We are doing what we normally do at the hospital—wait for things.) He is shaking and sweating. Straining to turn his head and look up at me with tears in his eyes, he says, *Don't leave.*

I'm not leaving. I'm right here. I stand next to him, holding his hand. *I'm not going anywhere.* I look over at the nursing staff, as if daring them to try and stop me. They don't. I start telling him about the chemical properties of Haldol, how it can cause this reaction in some people. He doesn't respond much. By the time the nurse comes out, his upper body is effectively paralyzed and his blood pressure is out of control. The nurse makes an emergency call to the doctor, and he is eventually transferred to a medical hospital.

When he is gone, I return to the dining room to rejoin the other patients, who had witnessed the event through the Plexiglas. One of them smiles at me. *Places like this need more people like you*, she says.

When you think about an adult with autism, what do you see? Have you ever thought about it before? I think to most people, kids with autism disappear into their adulthood, either by merging into society with the adaptive skills they've learned, or by being sent off to special homes or institutions. But as more and more of yesterday's kids become tomorrow's adults, there will be more adults with autism who don't fit into those categories. As a society, our view of what it means to have autism is changing.

By now, you may have formed a picture of me. What do I look like in your head? Are you content with what you see, your expectations of my personhood? Does it make you comfortable? Or do you want to know what I really am?

In the world of education, and indeed in much of scholarly discourse, it is taken as a rule that one must refer to an autistic person as a *person with autism*. This is called person-first language, and it is intended to, well, *put the person first*. Just as you are a *person with a dog*, a *person with a hat*, or a *person with pink hair*, this language posits that you can be a *person with autism*. A person with autism is not their autism; they are a person who happens to also have autism. The intention is to respect people with autism as human beings.

But to many autistics, this is not only wrong but also offensive. To frame them as a *person with autism*, thus extrapolating the person from their autism in the same manner as one may cavalierly separate clothing or hair color from one's core being, is a violation of their identity. To them, autism is not something that exists in a vacuum. It is something that has made an impact on their very personhood, developing them into the person they are. If they were not autistic, they would cease to be themselves. They would be someone else entirely. A different person.

A different identity.

    The question, then, is of the nature of fundamental personhood. Is the thing that makes a person themself to be understood as an ethereal concept, like a soul? Further, can a person be separated from their own life and boiled down to some essential component of themself, stripped of all other factors? Or is the accumulation of neural development and lived experiences into a visible phenotype, you, what it means to be the person you are? And how critical are those patterns of development and experience to the interpretation of the result, the person?

Insane Places

Dr. Pinball's office door is open. The small office is cluttered with books and papers strewn across every surface. A bookshelf, stretching the length of the room, is packed with countless volumes. Two sheets of paper are taped to the wall with a few names of people who had borrowed the professor's books scribbled down on them. Dr. Pinball is tall, over six feet, and perhaps he'd look menacing if his eyes were not quite so gentle from behind the spectacles perched on his nose.

He sits in a worn leather office chair. He says he *wears through chairs like a runner wears through shoes*. It's easy to see why: as he busily throws his fingers into the keyboard, he makes these full-body emphatic gestures, leaning back all the way and shooting forward to lean on his elbow. It seems as if the space afforded to him between the chair and the keyboard is not enough to safely contain the volume and velocity of his thoughts. This is something to which I can relate; I don't like to sit still, either.

Dr. Pinball *is* a clinical psychologist, but he's not *my* psychologist; rather, he is my teacher and my mentor.

My hands tremble as I hand over my discharge papers, a thick stack of crumpled sheets stapled together. My hands always tremble; it's a side effect of the lithium I am taking. Pushing his spectacles up on his nose, he says, *I noticed you were missing from class. I was concerned. How are you?*

I'm better, I tell him, staring awkwardly at my feet. I kick the tile floor with the heel of my sneaker. I'd been convinced, certainly, that nobody would have noticed if I'd died. Dr. Pinball's class was a lecture with almost two hundred seats.

But am I really better? I've been through this four times now. The first time you're discharged from a mental hospital, you feel like you'll never go back; the fourth time, you feel like it's inevitable that you will. How can I say *I'm never really better, I take six pills a day just to stay sane enough to be talking to you*?

The hospital ward is small, composed of two long arms attached to a central unit, the nurses' station. The nurses sit behind barricades of Plexiglas. This is 3 North, the adult dual diagnosis inpatient psychiatric ward, and I am dragged here involuntarily in an ambulance escorted by police. *Dual diagnosis* means mental illness and substance abuse. Double lucky. Some of the other patients are withdrawing from heroin or benzodiazepines like Ativan or Xanax. Me, I smoke a lot of weed. I am nineteen years old.

In the waiting room I listen to a manic woman who is coming down from crack cocaine; strapped to a chair, her sand-colored hair falling in disheveled strands around her shoulders, she looks at me with eyes that are all at once wide awake and asleep as she vividly recounts in a stream-of-consciousness fashion how she'd ended up in such a state.

Also in the waiting room is a kid I know from my days working in child inpatient psychiatry. I'll call him Pyro. He has a tendency to set fires wherever he goes, which is how he keeps ending up in these places. But if you ever ask him directly about it, he laughs and then smiles with this certain twinkle in his eye, and says cheerfully, *I don't set fires!*

Unfortunately for me, he is now being admitted to the same hospital as I am. When he sees me, he grins. *Elliot! Do you work here, too?!*

His mother eyes me. I laugh nervously. *Um. No. I don't work here.*

Pyro tilts his head in confusion and asks, *Then what are you doing here? Are you a patient, too?*

But before I can answer, he wrinkles his nose and turns to his mother. *What's that smell?*

I hang my head in embarrassment. I've been stuck in the limbo of the emergency room for three days, and there are no showers there. This is quite possibly one of the worst moments of my entire life. All I can think is that I can definitely never ask my supervisor for a letter of recommendation now. When I look up again, Pyro's mother is smiling sympathetically.

Pyro decides to talk to the older woman strapped down in the chair. He listens attentively for a minute and then starts asking questions: *Crack? What is that?* Then he turns to his mother and adds with a giggle, *Mommy! She said 'fuck'! That's a bad word!*

Pyro's mother looks absolutely horrified, but doesn't seem to know what to do. I decide to intervene in some manner. I am a mess, but maybe Pyro still respects me as some kind of authority, ostensibly; we've always had a good rapport.

I steady my resolve. *Hey, Pyro!*

He swivels and looks at me. His mother breathes a sigh of relief.

Come over here! It's been a couple months, right? What have you been up to since I last saw you?

Smiling with that twinkle in his eye, he says, *I haven't*

been setting fires!

Sometimes I feel like I am split between two worlds. Boy and girl; autistic and not-autistic; manic and depressed; even psychologist and psychological patient. Neither here nor there, this nor that; it's hard for me to feel like I fit in anywhere. It's always been hard for me to make friends. For my whole life, I've been an outsider looking in. A middle-schooler sitting on the playground with nobody to talk to. Sometimes it still seems like this is just the way things are, and there's no place left for me in this world.

Sometimes I feel like a ghost walking among the living. Is stigma something people can see, like a creature attached to me that's sucking out my life force? Does everybody know that I'm crazy, that I spent over a month in hospitals? And yet, if even hospitals can't really tell who is sane and who is insane, how can anyone be sure of themselves? How can I know? How can you?

I am hospitalized for the second time when I am eighteen years old. It is July, and at this hospital we are allowed to go onto a fenced-in area on the roof called the *rooftop garden*. It is disconcertingly like a cage, but as far as hospitals go it is fun; we make up games with a beach ball, a trashcan, and some hula-hoops. After a while of that, I'm sweating with exertion, so I sit down at the picnic table across from another patient, an older man with dark hair and a noticeable akathisia. He looks at me with his always-anxious eyes and asks, *So what do you do?*

I'm a psychology student in college, I say.

He nods sagely and then laughs to himself. *Psychology, huh? So what, are you doing an experiment on us?*

I reassure him that I am not. That said, I appreciate the spirit of his joke. It makes me think of the famous 1973 study by David Rosenhan, published in *Science* with the title

"On Being Sane in Insane Places".

It was supposed to be an experiment testing the reliability of psychiatric labels. Rosenhan sent *pseudopatients*—people with no history of mental illness—to emergency rooms and had them complain of hearing voices. Upon admission, they resumed their normal behavior. They showed no signs of any mental illness. And yet, all of them were forced to take antipsychotics in order to be released (in actuality, they flushed the medications down the toilet—no staff ever suspected this). Further, all but one were diagnosed with schizophrenia. Schizophrenia is, of course, a chronic and lifelong condition, not a transient one. The remaining one pseudopatient was diagnosed with manic-depressive psychosis (considered a more optimistic diagnosis), despite showing no evidence whatsoever of a mood disorder; coincidentally, this pseudopatient was the only one admitted to an expensive private hospital. So, in this regard, Rosenhan's experiment was wildly successful—he found that psychiatric institutions were exceptionally poor at telling whether someone really had a mental illness or not.

During their stay in the hospitals, which averaged 19 days but ranged from 7 to 52 days, Rosenhan's pseudopatients recorded evidence of dehumanizing and deplorable conditions. Pseudopatients reported pervasive invasion of privacy, utter lack of respect, and complete boredom. Staff regularly construed normal behavior as pathological and even rewrote patients' biographies to suit their diagnosis. Patients were routinely discussed as if they were not present, contact with patients by doctors was minimized, and doctor-patient contact averaged 6.8 minutes per day. The pseudopatients also documented several cases of verbal and even physical abuse.

Interestingly, none of the staff were documented as suspecting that the pseudopatients were imposters, but many of the other patients did have such suspicions: 35 out of the 118 of them, nearly 30%, openly expressed this. This is what the other patient's remark reminds me of.

Unfortunately, I am no imposter; I am not sane in an insane place. Rather, I am insane in sane places. But perhaps good can also be done by being insane in sane places.

In my own way, I would like to change something.

Elliot Gavin Keenan

Non Sequitur

I'm ten years old, and I'm about twenty-four hours into recovery from a tonsillectomy. I'm looking at my grandma's face on the TV screen. I'm never going to see that face again. They declare it a probable suicide by train and describe how the car exploded into flames on the tracks. I want to say, *don't you know that 'sixty-three year old woman' is my grandma? Don't you know this woman picked me up from school on Fridays, took me for bagels every weekend, never got shampoo in my eyes when she bathed me, made me chicken soup when I had the flu?* But they don't know. They'll never know, and they don't care. The depression starts around this time. The doctors ask me if anyone in my family committed suicide. I say *I don't know.*

I know it's wrong to tell lies.

In fifth grade, I want to die. In school I daydream about killing myself with an old circular saw in my garage, patched with rust and probably not even functional. Realistically, I am not able to even approach it—but the idea is somehow appealing. It looks very macabre.

I start to think about death often, and then I start to

think into other suicide methods. What if I shoot myself? Or hang myself? Or jump in front of a train?

I am sitting in a Brooklyn apartment staring at the wall. It is white and bare except for a painting, about two by three feet, of a naked woman cradling her head in her arms. Her face is turned away from the viewer. Her spine juts out above thin ribs as she curls into her knees. Blue shadows swallow her lithe and fragile figure; she is vulnerable.

Below the crying woman's portrait, a blue chair sits in isolation. R's bag has been left next to the chair. R's expression is one of deep concentration. She is writing in her journal, a daily ritual she conducts quite busily, each motion of her pen full of purpose. This is the manner in which she does everything: full of activity, a storm of motion clad in a thrifted black sweater. Her hair is short and brown and pinned back to make her look something like a swoon-worthy girl of the 1950s. She doesn't need to do this to get boys to swoon over her. She has no less than three dates lined up tonight.

I am not that way. I wear thick glasses and my favorite color is blue and I've only ever kissed one girl. It's odd for me to be in a place so far from home. This is R's world, not mine. I don't even like the noise of busy roads back in the suburbs where I live. There is so much noise here. Constant whirring and stirring interrupted by the dysfluent gurgling and impatient beeping of passing cars. I hear too much. Or do I listen too much? I am a collector of noise, a cataloger of sound, yet I am silent.

In the morning, R's bag is gone. I am alone in the Brooklyn apartment.

In kindergarten, one boy hits me in the forehead with a plastic truck during playtime because he doesn't want me to play with him. I cry in the corner. The teacher calls me up to the front of the room and asks me why I am crying, to which I respond, *I don't have any friends.*

She then asks my classmates to raise their hand if they are my friends. Everyone in the class raises their hand. But as I look around the room, taking in each of the children's faces, I am puzzled. None of them are my friend.

In middle school I get a locker in a special hallway for kids in special ed. Sometimes popular boys shove me into it and laugh as they pass by.

I fall silent around the time I enter seventh grade. I can still speak at home, or to my handful of friends, but at school I can say nothing at all. Sometimes I try to, but my voice goes silent and my palms get sweaty.

The other kids notice this change in me. Some girls in my grade make up a game; the object of the game is to extract the most pitiful squeak from me by saying the most absurd thing possible. The game is confusing, especially at first, because sometimes the girls offer me advice like *I think you should dye your hair blue.* Later on, when they can't stifle their laughter, I realize that they are hoping to lead me astray and do something they consider *uncool* so that they can make fun of me later with the other popular kids. I tell myself that I don't care what they think. But if I don't care, why can't I speak to them?

Maybe this is the beginning of my paranoia. Nowadays it often seems that my friends are trying to lead me astray, or that they are lying about wanting to be my friend.

I don't really remember the day I stop talking to DJ. I know it is winter and we haven't been getting along. I know that I'm starting to feel paranoid about him, confused about whether or not he secretly hates me. We don't talk for an entire semester. Then, the cloud of doubt starts to expand, covers my entire world: everyone is suspect. I spend most of my time in my room alone. I don't go to many of my classes. I know I smoke a lot of weed, I smoke three to five times per day. I start trading meal points for weed at some point. But I don't remember most of it at all.

There are lots of things I don't remember: like the time I actually did try to jump in front of a train. Or like telling everyone that I am failing my classes.

I know I did this, because on one Wednesday afternoon I am sitting across from my new psychiatrist. The office is disconcertingly like a hospital ward: you have to be buzzed in to see the doctors. My doctor is a middle-aged man with a funny haircut and a low voice.

We talk about my schoolwork briefly. I haven't even asked him about the intrusive thoughts I've been experiencing when he looks at me and says, *I've been reading your report from the psychiatric emergency room. According to the report, you said you were failing your classes. Do you remember that?*

No, I admit.

Do you remember what your grades for that semester were?

All As, and one A-.

I'm going to increase your dose of Abilify. The doctor nods and makes a note on his pad. *So let me ask you something: do you think that you were worried that you were going to fail, or do you think that you were convinced that you were failing and just couldn't get a handle on it?*

I know I must have really believed that I was failing my classes, because I even told Dr. Pinball about it.

I told you that you certainly weren't failing my class, he recounts. He is sitting in his chair. It's been replaced at least twice since I originally described it (he broke his other two.). *I figured it wasn't true, though you said my class was the only class you cared about and insisted you were failing the others. I knew you weren't studying and still doing well. But I could tell you were in this kind of state, so*

I told you to take care of yourself first.
>I frown, admitting that I don't remember any of that.
>*Is it hindering you to not remember?* Dr. Pinball asks.
>After a moment, I respond, *No.*

I know I tried to jump in front of the train. I don't remember it, but this is how I've reconstructed it in my mind. I make a dash out the door of my dorm. I know I might have worried friends on my tail, so I try to hide in a concrete hexagon outside one of the dorm buildings. I duck under the wall. My friends find me there and I make another run for it; unfortunately for my plans, I don't run very quickly. I'm clumsy and slow, and there are two of them. They restrain me and drag me back to my dorm room. The next day I'm admitted to the hospital.

>*So what did you do?* asks one doctor.
>I tell him that I tried to jump in front of a train.
>*That's inventive,* he remarks.

R eventually returns to the apartment to find me in a heap crying on the floor. She frowns. *Are you hungry?* She finally asks. I nod and pull on my boots and my coat. But I'm beginning to wonder about R, about our friendship. Does she really care about me? What if she's just using me?

Elliot Gavin Keenan

Liminal Spaces

Many of the kids in my school say that I am ugly. Ugliness, as I understand it, is a subjective quality; so perhaps the most accurate way to judge it is, indeed, by popular opinion. Therefore, I believe that I am ugly.

It takes me many years to understand that they are saying this, not because they think my face is aesthetically displeasing, but because I am transgender. Their qualms with my appearance are that I dress like a boy—I dress only in loose jeans and Pokémon t-shirts with the tags cut out—and that I don't shave my legs and that I am too fat. Even though I realize that this is the case, it doesn't answer the question of if I really am ugly.

My face has changed; it is narrower, and my jaw is dotted with dark stubble, and people no longer say that I am ugly. But I still think that I am sometimes; like when I would be kissing JS and I would stop and hide in the space between the pillow and the desk pushed to the edge of my bed. She asks me why I am hiding. There is a reason: I am too ugly to be with her. I don't want to say this, so I just say *no reason*.

I'm fourteen years old and I've squeezed myself into three sports bras, with the second layer folded up so that the elastic compresses the biggest part of my chest. There is a lingering chemical smell, some strangely synthetic floral scent hanging in the still air. I always arrive in the girls' locker room late so that I can be alone as I change into a black t-shirt and basketball shorts. I don't shave my legs; this draws glaring disapproval from just about everybody, including the teacher, who cavalierly suggests that I do. I slam the little blue locker shut and stand there for a moment, dreading the moment I step out into the gym.

It's the physical fitness test today. I know I can't run a mile, but every semester I am forced to try, scuttling along, a slow and clumsy excuse for a jog. This time I end up on the ground, sputtering for breath inside three sports bras.

I am in the first grade and standing on the playground, alone (as usual). Today I try to talk to a boy in my class. *I wish I was a boy like you*, I tell him. The boy raises an eyebrow at me. Then I decide that, being a boy, he must know how to become one. I decide to ask. Perplexed, the boy points to a tall, skinny tree in the middle of the playground. *Climb that tree,* he says. *Then you'll be a boy.* The tree's lowest branches are at least ten feet above my head. I sit down in the gravel at its base and cry.

I wake up after surgery. Bleary-eyed, I survey my surroundings: white and sterile, there is an oxygen mask shoved up my nose and an IV still attached to my arm. There is a dull, aching pain in my chest and what feels like a slight tug where two tubes fall out of my abdomen. For two weeks these tubes will drain brownish, yellowish, and finally clear liquid from my chest.

After the oxygen and IV are detached from my body,

I stumble out of the hospital and through the heat of southern Florida in July, into the car. The driver is a kind-hearted woman from the mid-west whom I'd only ever met at a writers' workshop. We rendezvous at the hotel with my other helpers, another woman from the writers' workshop and her sister, both originating from Tennessee. These people have been incredibly generous to me, coming across the country to do such a thing when my own family would not.

My school forces my parents to take me to a therapist. I've been depressed for at least four years, but I've never been to a therapist before. He is an older man with dark eyes, and the first thing he wants to talk about is my *gender issues*.
I want to be a boy, I tell him.
Haven't you tried just being a lesbian? he replies.
I don't know what to say to this. How does one *try* being a lesbian, especially when you can't get anybody to date you? The closest I had ever come to *being a lesbian* was when a girl in my class offered to let me touch her boobs for ten dollars. I said *no thank you*. And what does it mean to be *just* a lesbian? Is queerness like a game and you have to level your way up to being transgender? How many Rattatas do I have to defeat to evolve from lesbian to transgender? Moreover, I have no desire to be a lesbian, because lesbians are girls. This seems like a frankly obvious fact.
I leave with a prescription for Prozac and serious doubts about the quality of mental healthcare.

When I tell her that I am a boy, my mother blames it on my autism. True, there may be some similarities: a preference for loose, baggy clothing, particular interests that were often classified by the rest of society as masculine, and a certain bluntness to my social approach. I don't think that autism is a cause of gender nonconformity per se; interestingly, however, recent studies seem to indicate that gender nonconformity is more common in people with autism than in people without. But I am my autism. Of course autism is implicated in my decision to transition, because autism is the way my brain works. Autism is implicated in everything I do. So what if my gender is different, too?

Amphibios, as I've mentioned, literally means *both kinds of life*. In my childhood, I am fascinated with these creatures, primarily for their bright colors and odd appearances. But perhaps it is also because, like an amphibian, I am neither quite aqueous nor quite terrestrial; my existence is hard to categorize as male or female. I don't identify as a man or as a woman. Perhaps I am closer to a man, but I am different from most men. *Amphibios*. I am comfortable living this way.

After I leave the hospital for the fourth time, I decide to do something really tenacious. I am going to get surgery. I don't just want it; I am beginning to realize that, if I want to become mentally stable, I need it. I feel that I won't survive another year without it. I have to do everything in my power to get it if I want to live. And, for once, I do want to live.

My parents are completely against it; they refuse to support me either financially or during my physical recovery. Not only do I have to find over eight thousand dollars, but I have to find someone who would be willing to go to Florida for two weeks, and spend at least one week by my side twenty-four hours a day. I am going to need a lot of help.

I make a donation page and posted it to my Facebook. I don't really expect that I will get much.

Not long after its creation, word gets out to a community I belong to—instructors and graduates of a workshop called Alpha Workshop for Young Writers.

Alpha Workshop is a special place where, for two

weeks, a group of extremely talented teenagers and young adults workshop stories and learn skills relevant to writing science fiction, fantasy, and horror from New York Times bestsellers and longstanding names in the genres, as well as skilled up-and-coming writers, who are kind of like camp counselors as well as instructors.

I go to Alpha the summer before I head off to Art College. I am already starting to fall apart. I think that some of the other writers notice. I am very mercurial, quiet, and in general appear to be taking things really hard. At least one of the instructors tries to approach me about it, but I assure her that I am fine. I'm not. I'm not sure what they would do about it. I am seventeen years old and acutely suicidal, but this is not a new thing for me, and I'm not about to get kicked out of the workshop I've been dreaming of for months.

Especially at first, most of my free time is spent in my room, pacing up and down the hallway of the otherwise-empty suite. I make a few excursions outside to a very pretty-looking building, which is affectionately dubbed the fairy castle. I like that, so I go there, but I prefer to go alone. This is frowned upon.

Somehow, by the end of the workshop I know everyone, and I have made a few friends, although I remain a bit of a loner.

I remember everyone there fondly, and I leave wishing I'd been able to get to know them better. But I think I've missed my chance.

I certainly don't expect that one of my instructors would make a $700 donation and rally support from all of the other Alphans to find people to come with me on my journey. I find myself reconnecting with friends I never really knew I had. Not only are Alphans donating, but they are sharing the donation page, and writing all sorts of good things about me: that I am an amazing writer, that I am a mental health advocate, that I work with autistic children, and (most shockingly) that I am a good friend.

I raise over $1500 in donations in nine months—largely thanks to the community of Alphans.

I am in eleventh grade, and one of my classmates asks me what I want to do after college. He's presupposed, based on my academic aptitude and my now well-regarded intelligence, that I am going. This hasn't always been the case, but I have decided to get a bachelor's degree.

I'm going to be a writer, I tell him.

He scrunches his face at me. *Why? You're smart. You could be a doctor, or a lawyer. Something important.*

I shrug. *I don't want to be.*

With an incredulous look, he shakes his head and turns back around in his desk. The concept obviously baffles him—who would choose a career that would inevitably make them less money than their parents? But I don't care about that. I just want to be happy.

HILTON CHICAGO

I am sitting in Dr. Pinball's office. The discussion of the day is not purely one of science. Dr. Pinball is looking at me with that look, the *psychologist* look that lets me know he is evaluating the situation clinically. I don't tend to like that look in people; something about his, though, makes me want to trust him. There is a moment of long silence as he takes in my question and formulates his answer.
I believe you can achieve your goals, is what he finally says.
Me? There is a ticking sound; the clock on the wall.
Yes, he says. *You.*
I want to ask him why. I don't seem like a person to believe in. He would probably say something about how I had demonstrated an aptitude for academic work and how I had clear and ambitious goals and an intrinsically motivating interest in studying psychology; he's said those things before. But what I really want to know is, *How can you be so sure? What if, in the end, I'm destined for the state hospital?*

How I ended up in the hospital isn't easy for me to explain, not least of all because my dissociated brain can't seem to remember where I've been or what I've been doing. One way to express it is in the esoteric code language of the DSM: 296.6 (Bipolar I disorder, Most recent episode mixed), 299.80 (Autism spectrum disorder).

It's a miserable place. Patients don't get shoes. We get little socks with treads on the bottom that stick slightly when you walk. *Plop, plop.*

At this hospital there are two pay phones to the right of the nurses' station, which luckily do not cost money (I have been to a hospital where they did, and quarters were shuffled around like cigarettes in jail). During groups the phones are left off the hook, dangling by their metal tails, screeching dial tone into nothingness. Some people get calls every day. Others never get a single call.

I'm one of the lucky ones in that regard. My dad visits me almost every day while I am here. He brings me books (usually YA fantasy novels, as the print is just large enough for me to attempt reading), and we play my favorite board game, Settlers of Catan. The nursing staff look on in awe at the multitude of cardboard tiles, small wooden pieces, cards, and dice. I usually win against my dad. My friend DJ is the one who taught me how to play this game. DJ and I used to hang out all the time, until I stopped taking my lithium.

It is about six months after I've left the hospital that I realize I have lost time. Specifically, I have lost three or four months leading up to my hospitalization. Looking into this part of my past is like waking up sprawled out on a dorm room floor, trying to remember being blackout drunk. There are a few images, wisps of thread that once tied together something larger, something important, but the pieces are too sparse to resemble anything in particular.

I begin to search for clues, hints of what I was doing with my time, where I was, who I was with. Anything. Perhaps, if I can sort out the missing pieces, I will be able to construct a map back to myself. Back to before four hospitalizations, multiple suicide attempts, and six pills a day.

But so far, there is no map.

I do remember the hospital. According to my friends, I ended up there because I try to jump in front of a train. In the hospital, I get a package of letters written by my friends. They are all encouraging letters (one friend says *judging from the way you can hit a bong over and over, I think you can do anything*), written on printer paper with colored pencils. When I read them I begin to cry. I can see all of my friends reflected in their letters. Perhaps I haven't seen them properly in a long time.

My attending physician tells me that she is considering legally mandating me to take my medication or, worse, putting me on the list for the state institution. I know exactly how long that waiting list is because I recognize one of the other patients from my previous hospital stay, two months prior. And the state hospital itself is a long-term facility.

But, she says, *that's next time you end up here. I'm letting you go for now.* And she does.

Depression is an insidious thing. I am still discovering the extent of it. My depression has historically been so severe that it can be immediately devastating in every way imaginable, resulting in repeated hospitalizations. Nowadays it is milder, more a cold sting than searing frostbite, but it is an almost unrecognizable companion. It lacks the suicidal urge. It is more nebulous, a force draining my energy, motivation, and interests. This is thanks to lithium, I suppose; it has given me the ability to live, albeit in a liminal way. Lithium carries its own burdens with it: shaking hands, weight gain, a certain monotony of experience. Once you've experienced the free fall of a depression or seen the view from manic eyes, you don't know what it means to live within a normal human range of emotions. It feels like wearing a shirt that's too tight, constricting your range of movement. The drive to break free is instinctual.

In May, about a month after my fourth discharge, I am hired to work in Dr. Pinball's lab. I'm nineteen years old. Dr. Pinball studies autism spectrum disorder. I find research interesting, and of course I'm knowledgeable about the topic, but I've never been involved with research myself. I quickly find that my favorite tasks in the lab are on the computer: programming, organizing, and analyzing. I become adept in SPSS (a statistics program widely used in psychological research).

Under Dr. Pinball's mentorship, I begin to learn how to ask and answer research questions. I am fascinated with these lessons, and with the complexities of statistics that I am learning; I produce my own poster by the end of the summer. The poster is accepted to a conference in Chicago.

I am in Chicago, excited and nervous to be presenting my first scientific poster.

By the middle of the trip I am moody and volatile. I have a lot of conflict with my second and third authors in the hotel room. I am barely able to present my poster; I spend most of my time chain-smoking cigarettes outside the hotel, even though it is freezing cold.

Finally, the time comes to go to the airport and go home. I wait outside the Hilton for about an hour, and I am getting to the end of my patience; one of my coauthors is still inside, and he left me with his luggage. I start to walk back through the hotel so I can drop off his heavy suitcase. I decide I am going to leave his luggage there and start walking to the airport.

He meets me there just in time, and he's mad. I am, of course, even more frustrated.

And then he says it: *No matter what I did, you're just going to act this way, so I'm not going to say anything.*

It is like setting fire to a pool of gasoline. My neurons light up in just the right way and then there I am, making a dramatic exit and running off by myself in the wrong direction through the busy city streets of downtown Chicago.

By the time I am cooled off a little bit, the panic is beginning to set in. I don't know where I am. I don't remember how I got here. I stop, just looking around in confusion with my duffle bag and touristy Art Institute Chicago cap. I am standing there for a minute or two before I hear a familiar voice.

It is a PhD student and she is on the phone while heading in my direction. I pick out a few words of her conversation and I can only imagine that Dr. Pinball is on the other end. Clearly, she came to find his runaway research assistant.

She looks at me and hangs up, but doesn't quite put away her phone. I see her hand hesitate there like a finger on the trigger. To me, it seems she is preparing for the eventuality that this is going to end in a call to 911. My heart pounds. My hands tremble. Fight or flight. I struggle to stay in place. I can't afford to go to the hospital again.

The PhD student approaches me and asks me to walk back to the Hilton with her. I pause for a moment. Then I agree. Some of that visceral tension is beginning to dissipate, like a cloud of smoke fading into the November sky.

I am discharged from South Oaks after two weeks. Two weeks of tiny plastic cartons of orange juice from fucking concentrate. I gather up my books and my little journal and my handful of pens and put them into the big paper bag labeled with my name. In a second bag, identical to the first, I stow my sweatshirt (no hoodies, because they have strings in them), t-shirts, underwear, and pants. The nursing staff waves goodbye as I leave the ward through the locked double doors, lugging my belongings behind me. Their eyes are full of uncertainties. My dad comes to pick me up and we get my wallet and valuables from the safe downstairs.

Finally, I step into the noontime sunlight; it is April and there is a slight chill lingering in the air. The sky is somehow bluer than I remember it.

Certainly, before I had walked around seeing nothing but dull monochrome; and during my stay in the hospital, I'd gazed through the cramped windows and wondered, what would it be like if I could see that again, if I could remember who I'd been before this all began? But I couldn't. Even under the bluest sky, I could not remember.

At some point, I come to accept that I will not be that person again. That is, ostensibly, recovery. It is when I agree to swallow the pills, bite my tongue, and sit down in those painstakingly boring groups that I am allowed to leave the confines of the hospital's long hallway and its small, stifled courtyard. Even the grass there is fake, and when you lay back it feels itchy against your skin.

I cannot ever return to the bright daylight of my childhood.

Can anyone, really?

Three Desks to the Right

I graduate high school when I'm seventeen, and I go away to a small, arts-oriented college in Westchester. I'm a creative writing major. But when I am nineteen, I transfer schools, leaving my small college for a huge public university. I stop writing. It's hard to explain; writing has been an integral part of me since childhood. But I am in too much pain, and the fog that has settled over my brain from the medications I am taking makes it difficult to read.

A year and a half later, in the spring semester of my junior year, I pick it back up. I decide to enroll in a creative writing class. I am given the freedom to write on whatever topic I choose; so I start writing about the hospital, and Dr. Pinball, and everything I can think of.

The girl three desks to the right, JS, writes memoir too; she chronicles her experiences with alcoholism and schizophrenia. We become fast friends.

We are sitting in JS's car with the roof open, blowing tendrils of smoke out into the night. JS tells me that she wants to become a social worker and a therapist. I'm thinking that it's a wonderful idea; I picture a world in which people with mental illness become doctors and therapists. Then I realize that we are actively creating that world.

In my junior year, I win a research grant from the Autism Science Foundation. JS and I go to dinner the night I find out about the grant. It is around four-thirty, maybe, and the sushi restaurant is nearly empty. An older couple eats quietly across the room. Halfway through my spicy salmon roll, I notice that my hands are trembling so badly I can't pick up the next piece. I set them down and sigh, leaning back against the wooden bench. *Lithium*, I say, *You know how it is*. She smiles and reaches across the table, offering me her hand.

In it, I feel a slight tremor.

I am sitting next to JS at her kitchen table. It's her birthday today. I give her a book (a collection of poetry by mentally ill poets—*Poets on Prozac*) and a necklace, a flimsy gold-plated replica of oxytocin's molecular structure. Her therapist, whom I'd met earlier in the day (she insisted on shaking my hand), likes it. Oxytocin, the social bonding hormone, is the closest thing to love I know of in the language of neurochemistry. JS is wearing it now.

The cake has chocolate in it; after hearing that I am allergic, Mrs. S is determined to offer me another dessert food, eventually settling on fruit. I put a piece of watermelon in my mouth. JS is smiling. *This is the best birthday I've ever had,* she says.

I hold my gaze fixed on hers. I notice the color of her eyes. They are brown. I know this fact from pictures, but because I so infrequently make eye contact, I have never really seen it for myself. In the moment, I am vulnerable; I am entirely without a shirt. She traces the shape of the long raised scar across my abdomen with her fingers. After holding her gaze like this for a few seconds, I kiss her again.

I have never kissed a girl before.

I never eat except when I am with JS. Although I deny this, she seems to know; she always takes me to eat when she comes over, even if we only go to one of the school dining halls. She asks about it sometimes: *Have you eaten today*? And the answer is almost always *no*. I'm not exactly skinny, but I have lost weight, about sixty pounds in six weeks. This doesn't seem to worry anyone but JS. She insists that I am always fine the way I am. I don't know how to tell her that I am not fine. I don't dare ask if she would care if I were fat again. Even though I know what she would say, I'm terrified of the real answer, as if there is some unspoken truth hanging in the air between us; but I don't know if it's real, or if it's just my imagination.

The next day I return to JS's house for her family birthday party. Coincidentally, it's St. Patrick's Day. Grandma S watches me pile corned beef on my plate, insisting that I should take the last piece of soda bread. I eat it dutifully. (Later, JS follows me to the bathroom and stands outside the door, listening.)

Aunt Drunk arrives at the party with a six-pack. JS stiffens and anxiously fidgets with her phone. I know that JS' family religion is alcoholism. As her dad unearths another six-pack from the closet, we go into her room and hide.

We sit on the edge of her bed, a neatly made bed in the corner of a neatly organized room. She isn't crying, but I can tell by the look on her face that she is sad; maybe it is her silence or the way her mouth is pressed into a thin line or a certain downtrodden look in her eyes. We can hear Aunt Drunk's laughter through the walls. She hits her vape (she's trying to quit smoking), blowing raspberry-scented puffs of vapor into the still air. JS doesn't drink anymore, and to me it seems horrible that her family would bring alcohol to an ex-alcoholic's birthday party. I wrap my arms around her shoulders and we sit like this for a while.

Eventually, JS asks her dad to go buy some O'Doul's (a request that is quickly belittled by Aunt Drunk). She drinks three of them, still seeming uneasy.

One day, JS tells me a secret, something only her psychiatrist knows: she still hears the voices sometimes. I think I can tell when it's happening, because she gets kind of distractible and has this glazed look in her eyes, like she's really tired (and it does seem to happen mostly when she's tired). I ask her one day if she's okay to drive home, because she has that look, and she says yes; I don't question it, but I think she knows I know.

Sometimes, I wonder why I had to be born with an autism spectrum disorder. Why me? Why do I have to be the one who misses things, the one who doesn't know how to talk to people? Why am I the one who will always be alone in the end? What happened to make me this way?

One of the most currently compelling theories of autism's etiology concerns synaptic pruning. As babies, people with autism have a characteristic overgrowth of local connections in the brain. Everyone has this surge of connectivity in infancy, but people with autism have even more than normatively developing peers, and they're mostly connections within regions. Extra synapses are then pruned back and removed from the brain in childhood.

But in people with autism, too few of them are pruned, and so there is neural hyperconnectivity locally and perhaps hypoconnectivity globally as the connections between brain regions are less developed than the connections within regions. Almost all of the risk genes for autism are genes that affect this process of synaptic pruning.

One day, JS buys a picture book about Asperger's Syndrome. It's called *Inside Asperger's Looking Out*. The cover is a cute little raccoon, looking through a wooden fence; the pages are full of such photos, and are captioned with tidbits about life with Asperger's. The first pages read *OK, let's get a few things settled right from the start. People with Asperger syndrome are not broken, or damaged, or somehow less than 'normal' people. We do not need to be 'fixed', and we don't 'suffer' from Asperger's as if it is a disease. Sure, we may think and act and learn differently from others, but different can be a good thing.* JS sends me photos of these first few pages.

There is another disorder that, like autism, has a genetic component and features abnormal synaptic pruning. In adolescence, the prefrontal cortex is being pruned. This area of the brain is responsible for clear thinking, planning, and decision-making. Genetic abnormalities can tag the prefrontal cortex and other regions for pruning that is too aggressive. Important connections are lost. When that happens to someone who is at a high risk for the disorder, the symptoms of schizophrenia begin.

In a sense, then, autism and schizophrenia are opposites. One has too many connections, and the other has too few. One is hyper-logical, and one is hyper-abstractive.

But I think it's more complicated than that. For one, people with schizophrenia can weave elaborately logical tales to justify the perturbations of their world; a delusion is not purely chaos, but the person's attempt to make order out of chaotic perceptions. If you try to step into their world, you can understand the logic of that world. It just doesn't connect to reality.

To an untrained eye, the outwardly displayed peculiarities of schizophrenia and the eccentric behaviors of autism are not dissimilar. There can be mutism involved. And repetitive behaviors such as rocking back and forth can be shared, though for different reasons.

And then there's a degree of social inappropriateness. Either a schizophrenic person or an autistic person may act in ways that people find odd. In the case of an autistic person, it is likely because they do not understand or cannot accurately perceive what the social expectations are in a given situation. In the case of a schizophrenic person, I think something very similar could be true, although it is due to the general distortions of thought and not an inherently social deficit.

Poor eye contact, withdrawal, emotional dysregulation—the list goes on. There is some evidence that schizophrenia and autism share common risk genes. Not to say they are intrinsically related—I do not think this is so—but, in an external sense, they are sometimes similar.

As I've stated previously, prior to the introduction of *infantile autism* in the DSM-III, autism was classified as a type of childhood schizophrenia. This was largely owing to their phenotypic similarities: *Schizophrenic reaction, childhood type, with autistic features.*

She walks beside me, blonde hair glowing in the yellow wash of moonlight. I cough. She pauses and looks over her shoulder at me.

I, um, I was wondering, I stammered, *If I could, you know, hold your hand.*

She smiles that capricious smile. With full respect for the severity of my actions, she tries to stifle her immediate reaction and says *yes* and gently wraps her hand around mine.

Autos. Just as Dr. Pinball says in front of crowded lecture halls, it means *self.* Indeed, this term was originally used to describe schizophrenic patients.

I look at JS. Once merely the girl three desks to the right, she is no longer sitting three desks to the right, but beside me to my left. I want to understand her. What is this feeling called? Surely, this is the opposite of a self-ism.

Once, I was happiest by myself; but now I am experiencing some other kind of happiness, and its occurrence is correlated with the proximity of this girl to myself, as measured in desk units. I do not need a linear regression to tell me this. I can see the data points clearly in my head.

How strange, for two people who are supposed to be lost in their own worlds, isn't it?

Perhaps it has been a long time since I was last truly happy. I cannot remember it, but at some point it was so. I think it was when I was studying my special interests that I was most happy. It certainly pleased me to memorize the DSM-IV-TR criteria for every disorder in a chapter.

Currently, I am 296.65, which means *Bipolar I disorder, most recent episode mixed, in partial remission.* Partial remission means that subsyndromal symptoms are still present, or that the period of remission has been less than two months, or both; since my initial diagnosis of bipolar disorder, I have yet to ever meet criteria for full remission. But I'm working on it.

By some inexplicable mixture of circumstance and temperament, JS and I share a certain observational quality. We're good at observing behaviors. In my case, I do this because I lack some degree of automatic social intuition, and I must manually draw conclusions based upon discernible correlations; in JS' case, she does it because her intuition is an unreliable instrument and must be forcefully grounded in the evidently manifest, and therefore real, behaviors of others. This is, at times, a strength. JS is perceptive and caring. I'm caring, I think, if not incredibly perceptive. But observation is a process that takes time, and it has its downfalls. Lacking intuition leads me to make many mistakes; I often don't know, for example, when I am pushing somebody too far. I don't really have a mode that tells me I should be backing off.

It is a cool evening in the early days of spring and JS is sitting on a rocky ledge overlooking the main road on campus. I pace back and forth in front of her and stare hard at her face, noting the downwards trend of her mouth. *Are you sad?*

No, she says, and waits for me to try again.

As if it will make her emotions clearer, I squint and tilt my head at a roughly forty-five-degree angle. It doesn't help. *Are you... angry?*

She smiles very slightly at this. *I think you're moving in the wrong direction.*

Slightly flustered now, I sigh and seat myself on the ledge beside her. A car rushes by on the road below. *What are you feeling?*

Just tired, she says.

I have fatal flaws. I leave too many dishes in the sink. I freeload too many cigarettes. I'm too impulsive, and yet I think too much. I'm too open, and yet I'm too closed. I'm too weak, and yet I'm too strong. Worst of all, I don't know how to apologize.

Why is this? Perhaps I am afraid to forgive the faults in others. Do I judge too harshly, or do I view others in too strictly binary a fashion? Sometimes, by virtue of my flaws, I make other people angry or upset, and I know it's my fault. I have had many such failures in my life.

But if I am to forgive a person, and apologize to them, how would they feel? How would I know? For one, people in that situation don't tend to say how they really feel about it, and I'd be lost. And I'd be scared. What if they find my faults irreparable, as I find them?

There it is. I am not afraid to forgive the transgressions of others. I am afraid to forgive the flaws I see in myself. Perhaps I am even afraid to forgive my illness.

But if so many other people can forgive it —

Why can't I?

Elliot Gavin Keenan

Autism Diagnostic Observational Assessment

The ADOS is the gold standard in autism diagnostic assessments. I once help a PhD student practice for her ADOS certification by letting her do the assessment on me. It is kind of a special opportunity offered to me by Dr. Pinball (*I thought you'd find it interesting*, he says) and, as it occurs during the holiday season, I even see it as a weirdly suitable gift. There is nothing I like more than a good exam.

It is a module 4 ADOS, which is for verbally fluent adults, and module 4 has a lot of questions and just talking about things. The assessment is not hard. I talk about my friends and my feelings and my job. And then, at the end, there is our last activity:

Tell me a story.

How am I doing? I'll let you be the judge.

My friend BL is a professional autistic self-advocate. She is about my mom's age. Dr. Pinball said once that she is a good role model for me.

One day, we are discussing Dr. Pinball.

He hasn't fired me yet, I say. *He must like interesting people.*

Not true, BL replies. *Well, maybe true. But he keeps you not because he likes interesting people. He likes good people.*

Am I a good person? I don't quite know what to make of that. What does it mean to be a good person? Is a good person someone who doesn't hurt other people? If so, I'm not a good person. I've hurt lots of people.

Or maybe a good person is someone who always tries their best to help others, even if they end up hurting others at times. Do I seem like that kind of person to you?

It is a warm day in early spring and there are only a few wispy white clouds in the sky. The beachfront park is crowded with lots of people, especially children. The girl three desks to the right and I have just come from shopping in the village square down the street (she'd been interested in the tea store; in turn, I'd been interested in the board game store next door) and are now sitting at a picnic table eating some snacks I have brought along for just this purpose.

This is for you, she says. *It's mine, but I want you to have it.*

She hands me a book, in good condition but well-loved, with slightly worn edges. The book is *Look Me in The Eye* by John Elder Robison, a seminal memoir about life with Asperger's. I smile and thank her; truthfully, it is not only for the book, but for the fact that it appears to have been read multiple times.

I am six years old and I am alone in a dim corner of my living room, face illuminated by the harsh white-blue light of computer monitors. The sound of fingers hitting the keyboard fills the room. I am doing what I do best: writing. I don't have any real-life friends, but I play text-based roleplaying games on the internet with older kids. I spend many hours a day writing. I don't like going to school much;

the kids there are mean to me. Every day before school, one boy steals my backpack from against the fence on the playground where everyone leaves their backpacks and runs away with it because he knows I can't run fast enough to catch him. I am clumsy, uncoordinated, and very slow. I am in a special gym class, but my school is too small and only has one gym space, so the other kids see me doing gym, and they make fun of me. They call me things like *retarded*.

But in the high fantasy world of a roleplaying game, I can be whoever I want to be. I can be a boy or a girl. I can be short or tall, fast or slow, strong or weak. I can even be a dragon or an elf, or something of my own design entirely.

I tell my therapist about JS on a warm day in early spring. I am sitting in an uncomfortable green chair in her little office, a cramped room on the fourth floor of the psychology building. She asks about her diagnosis. *Schizophrenia*, I say, cautiously; *I mean, it seems well managed, but it is still schizophrenia.*

My therapist nods. *So what would that mean for you?*

I ponder this for a moment. The clock on the wall ticks. *It would mean that things could be hard sometimes,* I say. *It would mean that I would have to be there—but isn't the same true of me?*

Isn't it true of everyone?

Later that same day, I am sitting on a bench by the pond in the middle of campus, holding her hand. The pond's surface is black with wavering pools of yellow light reflected from the buildings nearby. *I saw my therapist today, too*, she says. *And she said that I looked happy, and that she rarely sees me without an undertone of sadness.*

My head rests against her body and I can feel her breathing. Gentle rise, gentle fall. We are lying in my bed. She moves slightly and I look up at her. My eyes meet hers, only for a moment, because even with her, eye contact is difficult. She smiles. It is a sad smile. *Do you have to leave to catch the bus now?* I ask.

She shakes her head and pauses, looking deep in thought. *I want to tell you something*, she finally says. I nod and sit up to face her. *Do you remember about what I told you—about what happened the last time I ever got drunk?*

Individuals with autism can have exceptional memories for facts and bits of trivia. Specific topics may be perseverated on; it is common to find people with autism who have expansive knowledge limited to areas of interest.

Of course I remember. I don't forget when someone tells me something like that.

That was the last time I've ever been kissed by anybody, she says. *Until I met you.*

I don't know what to say, so I look down at my blanket and I fiddle with it for a moment, and then I look back up and look at her. Her eyes are sad. *I promised myself that I would never kiss anybody again unless they were my best friend for life*, she says, more quietly this time. *I want you to be my best friend.*

I want to be your best friend, too, I say. But my hands start to shake.

Do you mean that? This is what they call a *rhetorical question*. She knows that I don't know how to lie. *Elliot*, she says, *I think we need to take things slow. Like, really slow.*

I am quiet for a prolonged moment. I don't really know what that means. What is slow and what were things and how long would it take for them? What is she trying to say? But what I actually say is, *Okay*. I look down at the blanket again. Then I glance at my watch. *You're gonna miss the bus.*

Are you okay? You look so sad. I don't want to leave you like that. She is staring hard at me. Maybe it is just a hard thing for me to understand.

Theory of mind is how one person understands another person's beliefs may differ from their own perspective; in other words, to put oneself in another person's shoes. This capacity is sometimes diminished in autism.

Yes, I lie.

Having autism is kind of like being colorblind to social situations. Instead of full hexadecimal colors—which is 16,777,216 colors—I see three-character hex strings. They are a decently good approximation of hexadecimals, but having only 4,096 colors, they lack some depth. Discrimination of shades remains difficult.

I retain certain characteristics of my autistic self, like an accent: monotone voice, poor eye contact, difficulty in relationships. There was a time when I was ashamed of these things. When I looked at the other kids, I felt jealous. The teachers had high expectations for them. They were going to be doctors and lawyers and businesspeople. Nobody called them retarded. And they had friends. I didn't. I wanted to be like them.

Somewhere along the line, my preoccupation becomes other people. In some ways, this catapults me into the social world; I am extremely smart, and now that I am motivated, I pick up some social skills with great agility. I am never quite as natural as the others, and I always seem a few years behind, but I am catching up. I become good enough to pass as normal.

But this preoccupation with people can be taken too far. People are not like species of frogs or chapters in the DSM; people can abandon you, and people can lie to you, and people can hurt you. People are not reliable sources of happiness, and they cannot be coerced into such a role.

I know this, but is it too late to change?

Children are like trees. Most of them grow straight upwards, towards the sun. But over the years my tree had grown sideways and twisted, ugly and gnarled and entangled in a thick underbrush. Could things have been different?

I refuse to be ashamed anymore. Every trait of mine is an *autistic trait*, because I am autistic. Even when my traits are obvious, their merit rests on a borderline between good and bad, valuable and dysfunctional. Honesty or irreverent bluntness, loyalty or bull-headed stubbornness, excitability and productivity or mania, passion or obsession. It's all a matter of perspective. Even intelligence, which is the trait of mine I prize most highly. It is a tool that has enabled me to live the life that I'm living, and yet at times it isolates me. I am smart and logical, but am I too smart and too logical? You can find the good and the bad in every person and every trait.

And so, I think I am not a good person or a bad person. I am both, neither, all of the above. I am complex. I am me.

I am sitting in Dr. Pinball's office. Dr. Pinball picks up a folder and says, *I just wanted you to know—and I think you already know this—that on your applications and in letters about you, even if it would be arguably beneficial to say that you 'can integrate personal experiences while navigating empirical literature with a precision I have rarely ever seen before', or something like that, I never write that you are a person with autism. And I do this out of respect for you—I would not want this information to be misinterpreted as if you have achieved things 'in spite of' autism.*

That's not the case, I said. *I've never achieved anything 'in spite of' autism. 'Thanks to' autism, maybe.*

Yes. I know that.

Then we talk about my ADOS results. According to the assessment, I have proficient mastery of language, my storytelling skills are quite good, and my reciprocal conversation skills are normative. But my eye contact is typical of someone on the autism spectrum, my vocal affect is somewhat monotone, and while I make ample use of gesture to describe things, I don't make many emotional, *emphatic* gestures.

I've never thought about that, I said. *But I don't think I'm going to start making more.*

Dr. Pinball shakes his head. *I don't think you should change yourself, Elliot.*

But do I still meet criteria? I ask.

I can't tell you that. It would be unethical. He pauses. *You already have a diagnosis, anyway. Why do you want one from me?*

I want to know if I outgrew it!

Dr. Pinball frowns slightly, looking confused. *Can you?*

According to the DSM-V, someone with autism can no longer meet criteria due to learned skills in adulthood. I want to know if I no longer meet criteria.

Ah. Dr. Pinball smiles slightly, as if he finds this funny. *I see. Well, I can't tell you that.*

Alright, I say, not too deflated. I will just have to decide for myself.

I stand and make my way to the door. As I stand there, in the doorway, I turn around and say with a smile, *I'm going to make an emphatic gesture.* I shake my fist.

Dr. Pinball laughs. *It doesn't suit you, Elliot.*

Art College

    I am sitting in a car with my friend, a mild-mannered young man from Russia who has just been diagnosed with bipolar disorder after a particularly rough hospitalization. He had called me shortly thereafter. When we meet up, he asks me a lot of questions, starting with *Should I go off my medication?*

    Of course I say *no*, and explain that bipolar disorder will return without medication, and could possibly get worse. *But*, I continue, *Almost everyone does try it at least once, so if you do, here are some tips.* And I tell him things like how you shouldn't ever suddenly stop and restart an anticonvulsant mood stabilizer, especially Lamictal, because you could get a rash called Stevens-Johnson Syndrome where the layers of your skin separate and you die.

    He nods. His expression is one of concentrated thought. *So I'm bipolar now. I mean, this is forever.* He looks out the window, into the foggy darkness on the other side of the glass. *But I wanted to be a scientist. Can someone who is bipolar still become a PhD?*

    I pause because I don't have a definitive answer for a

question like that. Maybe it depends on the person. What kind of person is he? What kind of person am I?

Why not? You can be bipolar and do anything, I decide and then add, *Unless it involves guns, like the military or the police force.*

He smiles. *They say Tchaikovsky was bipolar,* he muses. *And he was a genius. Maybe I'll be a genius, too.*

I am seventeen and in my freshman year at Art College, and I'm standing in front of my best friend PL's door at six in the morning to walk her to the gym. She opens it, frowns at me, and shuts the door in my face. A few moments later, she opens it again. *You're disgustingly chipper,* she growls.

At four the next morning I am on PL's dorm room floor doing several very uncoordinated push-ups because I am so full of energy. I've been writing lots of poetry, as the words seem to flow easily onto the page and I am suddenly able to rhyme like I never have been before. I walk around the campus at all hours of the night instead of sleeping. Often I walk in circles, with no destination in mind; to be fair, I have paced in circles since childhood, but normally I stop when I get tired. At Art College, I don't get tired. I love the moon and the snow, and I see this enchantingly pristine beauty in everything. I can't possibly close my eyes to go to sleep when the stars shine so brightly.

Later, PL tells me I get this certain look in my eye, and she knows that I am manic.

Despite having a good degree of insight, I sometimes make choices when manic that I regret. I write bad poetry, get angry at my friends over small things, and spend all of the money in my bank account on things I don't need. (This happens frequently enough that PL stops taking me to the mall altogether.)

One of the choices I make is to lose my virginity; specifically, to a stranger I meet on a hookup app. He is immediately rough with me, and I am scared, but it seems too late to stop. There is a lot of blood. I do my best to clean it up after, take a shower, and try to smile.

Then there are other times, often following the frenetic energy of mania; days when I sleep for twenty-three hours continuously, or when I gaze over the ledges overlooking the main road and wonder if I could ever find the courage to jump. Or when PL restrains me for several hours because I say I am going to kill myself.

It hurts my body to move, to walk, to do anything but lie in bed and sleep. During the time that I am awake, I think compulsively about suicide, or waste time carving thin horizontal lines into my left forearm with a shallow razor blade. I watch a single droplet of red blood roll down my fleshy white forearm. I can't really explain why I am doing this; I don't intend to die by this method, but I find it comforting somehow.

It is here, at Art College, where (thanks to a few appointments being moved around) I am finally diagnosed with bipolar disorder.

My therapist, Dr. C, is a good listener. After I get my diagnosis, she gives me a book recommendation. *I don't recommend this one to all of my patients, but I think you will like it,* she says. *It's similar to the way you think.*

I wonder how Dr. C knows the way I think about things, but she turns out to be right. The book is *An Unquiet Mind* by Kay Redfield Jamison. I have to get it from the school library, where it is on 4-hour hold for the abnormal psychology class. So I pretend to be a student in the class (I think this is what is called a white lie), pick up the book, run back to my dorm, and read it cover to cover in three and a half hours.

The following week, I tell Dr. C how much I liked the

book. She smiles at me. *Maybe you will write something like that someday*, she says.

I remember the time PL has to bring my clothes to the counseling center because I am being escorted by police to the hospital. I have never been hospitalized before; I am scared and crying. I can't sign the release because my hands are shaking. PL and Dr. C sit with me for a while until I am ready. The police and the ambulance are waiting outside. One of the officers taps his foot. I realize that no amount of waiting will make me feel ready for this.

Upon my arrival at the hospital, I am stripped naked and my body scrutinized; I try not to cry as I am examined. The nurse takes note of the fresh cuts on my forearm.

Sometimes I feel like there are two of me. As a student at State University, psychologists look at me and think I am probably some kind of genius, an accomplished young scholar. And yet, doctors look at me and think I am a broken shell of my former self. They see someone who needs to be kept behind locked double doors.

Who do you see? A good person or a bad person? A smart person? A sane person?

I once held the keys. I worked at an inpatient unit for six months. That person was me. When I was sitting there being told that I'd end up in the state hospital, that was also me. Maybe I'm crazy, but I have a whole life that I'm living. And maybe you're thinking that I'm the exception. But I'm not. People with mental illness are people. They come from every place and every walk of life. They all have a story.

RECODE (YOU = FRIEND)

I don't know how to apologize. When I am in second grade, the school psychologist tries to explain it to me. He is a very tall man and always wears a tie. *You should do something for them to show that you are sorry*, he says, looking at me over a wooden desk.

I look at him confusedly. *Like giving them something?*

The psychologist shrugs. *Well, maybe.*

I try the psychologist's advice, but it does not work. I don't understand this.

Dr. Pinball tries to explain it to me once, after Chicago. *It takes time*, he says, *And you have to demonstrate that you understand what you did wrong through your actions. But they may not want to be friends again right away. You may have to wait. And, sometimes, they may not ever forgive you completely; though, in this case, I suspect you have a good chance.*

As I understand it now, forgiveness requires two elements: effort and perseverance over a period of time. Perhaps you could say it requires an accumulation of social currency to attain forgiveness for a transgression. But what type of effort, and for how much time? This is where I have difficulty.

One day, Dr. Pinball's prediction comes true: my coauthors from the Chicago conference forgive me. I start by apologizing sincerely. After that, we slowly begin talking more, and after a while they ask me if I can help them on another poster that they are working on. They need help compiling and organizing the data, and since I am the one who created the compiling program, I am the only one available who knows how to use it. I show them, and then offer to continue helping them with organizing their data, because I know this dataset is difficult to work with. Of the members in their group, I realize that I am probably the most skilled with SPSS syntax. I actually really enjoy writing syntax. It's kind of like a puzzle. This is something I know I can do.

My former coauthor offers me an authorship spot on their poster for helping. I tell them I would be honored, but of course this is not why I offered to help them in the first place. What I really wanted to do was this:

RECODE (you=friend).
execute.

I think of Dr. Pinball's advice when I am trying to apologize to JS.

I don't want to fight. And I don't want to hurt her feelings. I know I hurt her feelings anyway, though certainly not on purpose. I need to show her somehow that I am sorry. So, this is what I know about saying sorry: it will take time, it will take effort, and it will take perseverance. I cannot control how much time it will take, but I should not give up any time soon. That is the perseverance element. And then, over that period of time, it will take effort. My best guess for what type of effort is something that would meet the following three criteria: something that shows sincerity, something that shows my intentions, and ideally, something that I am good at. Maybe even something I can do better than most other people.

What am I good at? I am good at board games, I am good at programming, I am good at writing, but none of those things will really help. I am good at research. I am good at knowing things. Perhaps. This does make some sense; after all, she had bought a book titled *Loving Someone With Asperger's Syndrome*. I could do the same.

I think of a conversation I'd recently had with Dr. Pinball, where he'd told me about an expert in pediatric bipolar disorder who had decided to immerse himself in the literature on sleep and became more-or-less an overnight expert on this topic, then changed his entire research focus to sleep research.

Truth be told, I feel that I could also be the type of person who can become an overnight expert in some new topic. And I can try to do this now. I decide to retrieve the book *Surviving Schizophrenia* (which she had mentioned to me) from the library, after checking to make sure it was in the main stacks, and to conduct a comprehensive literature review on the topic of relationships and schizophrenia. I decide that I will become an expert.

Sometimes, they may not ever forgive you completely. That's what Dr. Pinball had said. He was right. I hadn't hoped to find out the way that I did.

We are sitting in my room. I am lying on the bed and she sits in the middle of the room, and there is a desk in between us.

Let me ask you bluntly. Do you ever intend to date me? I ask.

She pauses for a long moment, and then says, *I hate to say this, maybe one day, maybe not. But not right now.*

Okay. I don't say anything else.

Are you okay?

Maybe... yeah. I nod sagely. *I guess... that I feel strongly about you, and maybe you have feelings for me, but we just don't have the same feelings, and so... I can't really pinpoint the moment your feelings for me changed. I thought it was going really well. Was it... my fault?*

No, she says. *It wasn't. And I do have feelings for you, and it was going really well. It's just... I was having just as hard a time as you were last week and, I guess, I just didn't like the way we communicated. So we just can't... be in a relationship.*

There is another prolonged moment of silence.

I like you too much, I say. *I think... the things that make me a good person, are also the things that make me a bad person. I'm honest, but I'm too honest. I told you how I was feeling. And I told you I loved you. I'm loyal, but I'm too loyal. I love you and now I can't change my feelings. I can't go back. Every time I'm next to you, I think of things that happened in the past. Kissing you... was really big for me.*

She sniffles. *I know. I'm sorry. I'm really sorry.*

My feelings for you are... how should I say this? Very... pure. I can't hate you. And I don't blame you for anything, honestly, I love you.

Look at me, she says.

I look at her over the desk. Her eyes are red. She is crying.

You know... I love you. I want to make you happy. But if I can't be that person—if I can't make you happy, then you should be free and find someone who can. So... it's okay. I am sad... that I could have these feelings for someone, and they can't accept them. I am sad.

I hear a muffled sob from the other side of the desk. I sit up and swing my legs around the edge of the bed, put on my hat, and stand up. *Maybe you want to go home now.*

She nods silently and then says, *I feel like the worst piece of shit person ever. My heart is shattered into a million pieces.*

By me?

She shakes her head. Her hair is tangled, bits of it stuck to her face by tears. *No. I don't know. By everyone.*

I hand her a box of tissues. She needs them. Her face is contorted by sadness. *It's okay. Everyone breaks someone's heart.*

Again, she nods, and sniffles. *Okay... well, I should go home. Goodbye...*

Goodbye. I am calm. I am not crying.

With another sob, she walks out and swings the door shut behind her.

Can you love someone while still trying to completely understand them? I wonder, sometimes, if I truly understood JS. Certainly I tried; I listened, I talked to her often, and I read all of the books she recommended and more. But I did love her. I do love her.

Memories fade. Mine certainly do. This is something I've learned to be true for anyone. But you can engrave certain memories onto your heart, and keep their essence with you for a long time, maybe forever.

Now that we've said goodbye, I must choose what memory to keep. Will I carry with me hurt, or anger? Will I remember the tears, salty and burning in my eyes from too much lithium? Will I remember holding the broken pieces of my heart, and trying to glue them back together?

No. I don't choose to carry any more misery in my heart. This is what I will engrave:

A warm spring day at the park. A sunny pier, and a shady gazebo. The ocean rumbling slightly beneath our feet. Our eyes meet. The first time my lips touch hers. The taste of her tongue. I have never kissed a girl before. I am nervous. My heart pounds in my ears. My hand finds her shoulder. She smiles.

I put away the book she gave me.

They say the cherry blossom is one of the most delicate flowers. It blooms for only two weeks in the early spring. It can only survive at precisely the right temperature.

Goodbye, JS. Goodbye.
It is the saddest word in our language.

MATTITUCK 205

I am sitting in a sparsely occupied dorm room on the Southampton campus, on a Skype meeting with Dr. Pinball, and he asks me how the writers' conference is going. I arrived a couple of days prior. Thus far I have only been to one class, and I haven't really made any friends, but I am still hopeful.

It's good, I tell him. *Writers are strange. I was sitting here painting and my neighbor was… playing the banjo, I think.*

Dr. Pinball laughs. *That doesn't surprise me at all.* He pauses and looks to be in thought, possibly reflecting on his time with his college ska band. *Artists and scientists are, well… I think you're about to experience the differences between those two worlds first-hand, Elliot. It will be interesting for you, I am sure.* Then he laughs again.

Truth be told, I'm missing JS. We registered for the summer class together, but she doesn't show up; our teacher mentions that a seventh classmate dropped out at the last minute. So there are six of us now, me and five other creative writing students I've never met before. I don't know why this makes me so sad. It's not as if I was expecting her to show up. Maybe I was hoping for it.

The next day, I am standing outside the building where classes are being held, smoking a cigarette and talking to a boy in my class named L. He has sandy blonde hair and always dresses in all black even though it's July. I am telling him about my own diagnoses and he starts to say *I have, um...* and then stops, stealing a glance around the area, and says, *Well, nevermind.*

It doesn't take much for me to notice that there is something a little unusual about L. His affinity for conspiracy theories is probably pathological; he increasingly hints at strange beliefs about aliens and a variety of government conspiracies. He is paranoid about a lot of things, especially the police.

We are walking down the highway in Southampton just off-campus, passing a joint around, when he stops and mumbles something about someone following him.

I think you're good, man, I tell him. He looks around again, and then puffs on the joint.

We're sitting in L's car and driving back to campus from the town of Southampton on the highway. L confides that he was hospitalized for an acute psychotic episode, which was labeled as single-episode mania (296.04: Bipolar I disorder, Single manic episode, Severe with psychotic features), and that he is being maintained on Zyprexa (an antipsychotic drug).

I already know that his symptoms don't fit a typical manic profile, nor are they single-episode. But I'm no clinician (yet). I listen to his story, nodding.

Then L glances over at me and asks, *So you're bipolar. Is there such a thing as bipolar disorder with, like... without the bipolar?*

I look back at him confusedly. *What do you mean?*

Like, I don't know... without the bipolar episodes.

I don't really know what to say to this. I do not know how to tell him; there is the distinct possibility that an insinuation his beliefs are pathological in nature could be met with hostility. I want to be an ally, not a harbinger of any kind of destruction. It feels like the best thing I can do is to be his friend.

Still, I think of JS, and can't help but feel that the friend L needs isn't me, but her.

It is a Sunday night and L and I are smoking outside our dorm building when an acquaintance of mine from the conference walks by, smelling faintly of alcohol. Her name is JG. Like me, she is writing queer bipolar memoir. We often run into each other smoking in the middle of the quad (a patch of faded, sun-bleached grass in between the cluster of dorm buildings) and we chat about many things going on at the conference. At this venture, she tells us she is heading back to Mattituck, where there is a party going on. She invites us to join her, and of course I say yes, which means that L is along for the ride.

So there we are: me (by invitation, I am sitting in the designated reading chair), L (who is constantly looking about the room), JG, three other writerly women who are probably all in their thirties, and one very drunk writing professor. I'll call her Professor Writing Fairy.

Professor Writing Fairy is lighting a one-hitter while I read a few scenes from my memoir. Everyone seems very impressed by *the clarity of my prose* and the fact that I am an undergraduate. I hold back on congratulating myself, as they are all a little tipsy.

After I finish my reading, L and I decide to grab his weed and my bowl from our respective rooms. Professor Writing Fairy and JG come along with me as I retrieve my supplies. They marvel drunkenly at the self-portrait I had painted earlier, which is now hanging on my door, and then we return to the party.

About half an hour later, everyone is stoned.

Professor Writing Fairy looks at me and starts gushing something about how I am really smart and attractive and meeting me was like *a meeting of the minds, like a brain connection,* but I am experiencing an auditory processing delay and I can't quite keep up with her garbled speech, so I just nod and follow along as best I can.

Then she goes on some kind of soliloquy about how she wants me to give her the time of day, to which I confusedly ask, *You want the time?*

The time of day! she says, quite urgently.

I glance at my watch. *It's 11:37.*

There is a moment of silence and then everyone else in the room bursts out into laughter. Professor Writing Fairy seems to think on answer [ANSWERING?] this for a moment, and then says profoundly, *Nobody has actually ever given me the time before.*

Writers, as it turns out, are interesting people. It is also interesting to be characterized by another writer. JG and the others at Mattituck describe me as being like a real-life Charlie Kelmeckis from *The Perks of Being a Wallflower* (*he sees things and he understands*, says JG).

Two days later I am invited to a second Mattituck party. This time it is a prompt party, and the first prompt I get is to write five six-word memoirs. I dislike the X-word story format, maybe because I think most of them miss the point, so I groan a little bit. After some deliberation with myself, I write the following:

Seven years old. Psychiatrist watches me.
Silence. Children point and laugh. Silence.
Body inspection. "Shallow cuts on forearm."
Fourth discharge doesn't feel as special.
3 months. Silence. Loving you still.

After the prompts are over, I am showing a (yet again) drunk Professor Writing Fairy my one-hitter. I point out the lipstick stains, a smudge of pink around the tan ceramic edges, that so clearly remind me of the one-hitter's original owner.

I wish I could absorb the lipstick stains out of your heart! proclaims Professor Writing Fairy. And then she says, *You know, I think that you shouldn't put guilt on yourself, I mean it sounds like she has some serious things going on.*

Getting advice from the older writers (since I'm the youngest, they all feel compelled to dispense life advice to me) is often not like getting advice from a mentor like Dr. Pinball, but from an older version of myself. In a way, this is very useful insight.

Perhaps JS was just the wrong person for me to surrender all my trust to. This doesn't mean that either of us are bad people. It means that we were bad for each other.

I decide that when I am ready to believe that, I will.

As usual, L and I are standing outside Mattituck smoking a cigarette. He starts telling me in more explicit detail about his psychotic episode, and then rather doubtfully about his subsequent bipolar diagnosis. Then he takes a long drag. His question surprises me. *Is it true that, you know, all schizophrenics are bad?*

No, I say. I pause for a moment and ash my cigarette onto the concrete. *You know, my ex-girlfriend, the one I've written about, is schizophrenic. She has it pretty together. I mean, it's not easy, but it's not impossible. And I loved her, I mean, a lot.*

He nods. *Thanks.* He looks a little relieved.

We are taking a walk and smoking a spliff down a side street near the campus. It's L and I, and another classmate, PB, who describes himself as aspiring to be *the Carl Jung of our generation, mixed with a little Maslow.*

We are talking about the types of books we are going to write in the years to come, though as high conversations tend to do, the topics shift fluidly into something tangential. *I have a theory about how we could provoke the rapture, you know, if it's real,* says PB. *But I gotta convince all the people of the world to self-actualize first.* He looks to be deep in thought.

It is nice to have writerly friends, especially since feeling the loss of JS. We had once partaken in conversations like this—well, not like this, but like this with more sobriety. JS had convinced me to get sober for a while, actually. I suppose it didn't stick. We are very different people, in the end, even if we are very much the same.

Later, my classmates and I are having a smoke outside and discussing the causes of anxiety. L is convinced that aliens are to blame, PB discusses at length how it is the ego that creates anxiety in the mind, and I stand there quietly thinking about how it is probably amygdala overactivity and a so-called imbalance of neurotransmitters in the limbic circuitry. Of course, the conversation then flows into PB's desire to create a network of what he deems to be profound individuals, and how we all should be included.

I'm not very profound, says L nervously.

You're pretty fucking profound, I contest.

Yeah, you're profoundly different, PB adds, rather admiringly.

PB explains Jung's concept of synchronicity to me at some point. As I understand it, this is a connectivity between statistically uncorrelated events (coincidences, as you might say) that creates meaning. I think that my life, and especially my memoir, is full of synchronicity; and indeed, perhaps this is how I instill a sense of orderly meaning into my life—by connecting together uncorrelated events, and especially uncorrelated people.

I think synchronicity is the backbone of artistic creation, I conclude.

That's very profound, says PB.

I don't remember exactly what I said the last time I texted JS, which I have come to realize means that I probably said something I don't really feel. I remember that she was angry at what I said, at least at first. She also seemed to realize that it wasn't in my control. And at that, I guess, she probably felt kind of despondent. She isn't a person who is lacking in resources, but the resources she does have are (like mine) frequently full to capacity; she couldn't afford to have someone like me, who would unpredictably spout various forms of toxicity. If I really couldn't control it, there wasn't a whole lot of hope. And maybe that is why she was crying.

I think I can understand sadness in this context. It arises from a mismatch between your hope for a situation and the reality of it. I can only imagine that for her, giving up on someone because of their mental illness was a very hard decision. Maybe she even had feelings for me.

As for me, I still feel sad, but I'm getting better.

I know that I have identified synchronous events in my life. For example, despite their vast differences (I thought of L's crumpled cigarette packs with the tops torn off, compared to JS's rather well-kept ones with crisp edges, and this is an apt metaphor of their general impressions), both my ex-girlfriend and my new friend are twenty-six year old schizophrenic writers who smoke like chimneys, and I'd met them in chronologically adjacent classes; at this point you'd think that I am in the habit of seeking out this very specific brand of company. Despite the reality that it was coincidental, to me, it was meaningful.

I don't really believe in fate, but that's the psychological tendency of synchronicity. And maybe it is the reason I write.

Elliot Gavin Keenan

Cognitive Tunnel Vision

My research focuses on comorbidity, which is what happens when you have two or more disorders co-occurring. Comorbidity is an interesting problem, because there are many ways to conceptualize it, and each combination could have a different answer as to which way is the best way. For example, if a person has Diagnosis A and Diagnosis B, this could mean:

They have a straightforward case of Diagnosis B on top of a straightforward case of Diagnosis A. The two constructs are independent, and the result is merely equal to the sum of its parts. This is the simplest way to think about it.

Diagnosis B is an atypical presentation of Diagnosis A. In this case, then, Diagnosis A is causing the symptoms of Diagnosis B.

Diagnosis A and Diagnosis B together are something else entirely, therefore representing a Diagnosis C. This is an unusual way to think about this problem, but there is one clear-cut—albeit flawed—example of this in the DSM, which is schizoaffective disorder. In the simplest terms, bipolar disorder plus schizophrenia equals schizoaffective disorder bipolar type. Or, depression plus schizophrenia equals schizoaffective disorder depressive type.

(Schizoaffective disorder is not well-defined, however, and I think it represents an anomalous categorization; there is no other diagnosis that I can think of that is a combination of two other disorders, and there is no reason that I know of to consider depression plus schizophrenia more special than depression plus anything else. Its anecdotally apparent decline in popularity as a diagnostic label may be an example of something called diagnostic drift.)

There are other ways to think about this, too—like the way I think about autism plus depression in my senior thesis, which is that they are independent constructs, but symptoms of autism (repetitive cognitions) place an individual at greater risk for developing depression, so they are separate but linked. My thesis project endeavors to establish this link between autism and depression via repetitive cognitions.

I see her face in a dream. I've never seen anyone's face in my dreams before. I have congenital face-blindness; whenever I see someone I know in a dream, their face is blurred out. I rarely even notice this because I don't make eye contact, even in my dreams. But for the first time in my life, I notice someone's face looking back at me in a dream. And it is hers.

I am speaking on a panel at an autism symposium in New York City. BL got me this job. It is a relatively small symposium, with an audience of about two hundred people. They are all well-dressed and I think many of them must be very wealthy. Waiting for my panel, I make friends with a well-known researcher sitting next to me at the presenter table.

The panel I speak on is about dating, gender, and sexuality in young adults with ASD.

One audience member asks, *What advice would you give to a young adult with ASD who wants to date?*

I consider my answer for a moment. I know I want to say something genuine, but also something practical that will not only appease the typically-developing audience but make functional sense for a person on the autism spectrum.

I think, for people with ASD, some of our differences can be our strengths, I say. *So if you're like me, you might be good at remembering things that interest you, really good at researching and collecting information you've prioritized. So my advice, if you're having trouble connecting to your partner, is to prioritize information that is relevant to them. Do some research—something you're good at.*

The moderator of the panel, a world-renowned expert on the topic at hand, smiles widely at me. *Wow*, she says, and then looks out to the audience. *I bet everyone wishes they had a partner with ASD now.*

I smile, a bit of sadness weighing down on me. If only.

At the end of the panel, a lot of people come up to me to ask for my contact information. One guy asks if I'd be interested in speaking at a big conference in Philadelphia. Somehow, my career as an advocate has begun. Indeed, I am proud.

I'm not allowed to walk to middle school. We live across town and my parents are afraid that I might get lost on my way there, or be hit by a car crossing the road. So a bus comes to my house every morning and drives me to school along with two other kids: one girl with childhood-onset schizophrenia and a boy with autism. Indeed, it is the infamous *short bus*. This one is the only small bus in the whole school.

The girl always offers me a nervous smile, though few words are ever exchanged between us. She very rarely speaks to anyone. I know she can speak, or at least understands speech, because she answers direct questions with silent nods or little *hm*s. A few times I see her break down and cry with no apparent antecedent at all. Other times, she smiles slightly and laughs at nothing that I can see. I often wonder what she is thinking about. Very frequently she has this slightly clouded look on her face.

Her manner is usually gentle. We are bowling in the hallway during our gym class (which is just the three of us and our teacher), and she is on my team; I throw the ball sideways and it deftly avoids any of the pins.

Sorry, I say, embarrassed.

In a near whisper, she responds, *It's okay*. She smiles at me.

By the end of eighth grade, the crying fits have become more frequent and more destructive. She transfers to a special school. I never find out where.

Unlike the girl on the bus, the boy is quite vocal, sometimes excessively so; he talks endlessly about trains (he memorizes the train schedule and rides his bicycle to see the trains going by) and music. After gym, I watch him go up to a group of the kids in my honors class and try to make conversation with them. My academic classmates are very different from me and the kids on the bus. They laugh at him. He looks a little confused, clearly trying to understand the joke.

I am standing on the sidewalk outside the emergency room. My duffle bag is packed. Clothes and a notebook and pen. No strings, no elastic. I am ready.

But I'm staring at those blaring red letters attached to the hospital's exterior—EMERGENCY—and I think them a little too urgently shouting for my needs. I am not an EMERGENCY, shouting and sirens, I am more like a slow, smoldering burn. A slowly fading whisper: emergency, emergency, emergen…

I look at a picture of JS. Though I once knew, by now I have pretty much forgotten what she looks like. In this moment, I want to remember. I will forget in time.

I look up at the sign again. EMERGENCY. It seems to stare back at me.

Is the psychiatric emergency room the place where I must go to wash myself free of guilt, to expunge myself of sin? Is this place my temple? My safe-haven?

There is nothing left to settle between her and I. I know that. There is only something left to settle within myself. How do I even begin to settle such a thing?

I'm highly perseverative. I think it's hard to understand what this really means. Phrases like *perseverative thinking* and *circumscribed interest* conjure images of an autistic child lining up a sizeable collection of toy trains or obsessing over a certain period of history or memorizing every detail of the periodic table. And indeed, I was very much like this, and still am (after all, when I was a child I memorized lists of diagnostic criteria from the DSM-IV-TR); but I think the underlying thinking style is more complex and maybe more problematic than that.

It seems sometimes that almost all of my problems come from thinking too much about something bad, like my head gets "stuck" on certain topics and can't move on. And if something is uncertain or unresolved, it makes it all that much more difficult to get unstuck. My therapist has tried to help me with this issue. The best anyone has come up with is to distract myself by staying busy. When I slow down, the unwanted thoughts return. I can't stop thinking about things I don't want to be thinking about. It feels like I can't control it.

There are times that I wonder if people are incredulous when I tell them that I have autism. I can't really tell, although

I know some people do act surprised. Once I tell my friend's housemate that I was in a special ed class.

He nods. *Like an inclusion classroom.*

No, I say. *It wasn't an inclusion classroom.*

He pauses and looks at me confusedly. *What do you mean?* So I think it may not be evident.

I don't wonder this due to fear, but merely out of a wish to be understood. Perhaps everyone wishes this. If people don't know I'm autistic, or don't believe it, I worry that they will misinterpret some things that I do.

I am autistic, so autism is present in everything that I do, even if not eminently recognizable: like the way that I walk, slow and slightly dragging; the intonation of my voice, a little bit monotone; the syntax of my sentences; the way my gaze shifts away from people's eyes; even the way that I write.

However, when people talk about autism as if it's a negative trait, or even worse, as if it's something to be feared, I am a bit confused. There are parts about myself that I dislike, parts of myself that are hard to tolerate, but they aren't necessarily those parts. Some of my best qualities are associated with autism, ostensibly. I have had difficulties, but I don't resent autism for that.

In fact, every characteristic of me is an autistic trait, because autism is neurodevelopmental. Autism is my brain, and my brain is me. So maybe every terrible thing I have done, my mistakes, are somewhat attributable to autism, but so too is every wonderful thing I have ever achieved. I cannot hate autism. To hate autism would be to hate myself.

I don't always like being myself, but I believe that I am necessary. There must be people with my traits in the population. I wouldn't wish to *cure* autism as if it were a disease. I am not a disease. I have made many mistakes, but I am not a mistake.

Although I still have unusual traits, I've changed a lot

since I was a kid. For example, I used to cry every time I had to sit on the left side of a car. But now I have a learner's permit, which means I have to sit on the left side of the car, and I don't cry when I am driving. I also used to cry every time I had to go to the department store with my parents, because the lights made a high-pitched buzzing sound that hurt my ears.

And I have an aversion to saliva. I've never shared drinks with anybody, not even my mom, and I don't eat food if someone else touches it once it's on my plate. But once, at JS's birthday party, she didn't want to blow out the candles because there would be spit, and I asked her if she wanted to blow out candles on my piece because I said I didn't mind. And she said no. But I really didn't mind. I'd already touched the inside of her mouth and I did not find this objectionable. I suppose I would have shared drinks with JS, too, although I do not think she would have asked this of me. Maybe this is a metric by which I judge love.

But enough about that.

The smell of cigarettes used to make me feel sick, but they don't anymore. I have less sensory sensitivity than I used to. Perhaps this is correlated to my level of social functioning. Certainly, I have become much savvier since I was a child, and I smoke quite a bit now, especially since seeing JS—I had never smoked that much before. (Interestingly, there is scientific literature concerning the smoking habits of people with schizophrenia. It is unusually common. Most likely, it has to do with dysfunction of the nicotinic acetylcholine receptors, leading to cognitive impairments that are alleviated by nicotine.)

Me, I'm just good at picking up people's vices.

I am sitting in Dr. Pinball's office and we are talking about my senior thesis. My thesis is about perseveration in autism and its relationship to depression. *I was thinking the other day that this is similar to something you experience,* Dr. Pinball comments. He seems amused by this. *Well, they say most research is 'mesearch'.*

I agree with him, as I know this is the case. My inspiration for the idea had indeed come from self-observation. I don't think *mesearch* is a bad thing. I don't think Dr. Pinball thinks it is a bad thing, either.

Dr. Pinball has told me a few times now that my struggles are all a part of my research training; *You have different strengths than other people,* he says. *I don't have to teach you how to read an article. You just have different things to work on.* Then he adds, *I was the same way.*

Dr. Pinball has said a few times things along the lines of *I was once a lot like you, Elliot* and I've often wondered what exactly he means by this. It is a rather vague statement. There are a lot of ways somebody could be like me. Does he also have three cats or curly hair or a great fashion sense? (I know the latter is not true—Dr. Pinball would not be offended by this, as he admits he does not know what it means to *match* colors. I tried to explain color theory to him, but he did not seem to understand.)

I assume Dr. Pinball does not mean any of those things.

April 4th, 2016. One year since I left the hospital.

A few white snowflakes tumble through the muddled sky. When they hit the ground, they melt away and disappear. It has been a good year. Three scientific poster presentations, two conference appearances, and work beginning on my independent honors thesis project funded by one prestigious grant from the Autism Science Foundation.

One year ago today, I was discharged from the hospital. It has been one full year since the day I last sat in that gloomy small courtyard, feeling that itchy fake grass, looking up at the blue sky from the perspective of a caged bird. I have been working on a lot of things in the process of putting the pieces of my life back together.

My friends have forgiven me. Have I forgiven me? Have you?

I don't know. But I did find my map.

It wasn't the map I was looking for. It didn't lead me back to my past self; but it did lead me forward, to my future self. To find the map, I had to find my voice.

What I'm trying to say is this: in writing about myself, I drew my own map.

Where does it lead?

Elliot Gavin Keenan

INTERNATIONAL MEETING FOR AUTISM RESEARCH

The day after I try to admit myself to the emergency room, I visit Dr. Pinball's house for a lab party. When the party starts winding down, Dr. Pinball invites us into his living room and shows us remnants of his college-age musical career, starting with a video of a jazz mashup version of *It Wasn't Me* by Shaggy.

One of my colleagues notes that Dr. Pinball plays the saxophone with the same level of energy and enthusiasm that he brings to research. We all laugh because it is entirely true. Dr. Pinball on stage is very much the same Dr. Pinball who has a habit of breaking office chairs.

This makes me think... that I don't regret anything that I've done, I say. *You know, like, writing a memoir.*

Dr. Pinball laughs a sort of big laugh and says with a smile, *Nor should you, Elliot.*

The International Meeting for Autism Research (IMFAR) is held annually. I am in Baltimore, ready to present another poster. It is somehow amazing to be surrounded by people whose names I've read in articles, many of whom are truly renowned experts in the field. At the opening reception, I make accidental eye contact with Dr. Cathy Lord, the creator of the ADOS. (I promptly run away. Some part of me is a bit afraid that she might have some kind of super ADOS-vision.)

Dr. Pinball introduces me as his *star undergraduate* to seemingly everyone he talks to, and always mentions my Autism Science Foundation grant. He seems proud.

On the second day of the convention, I am taking a break and sit charging my phone. Two men sit down quite near me. I listen to them talk while scrolling through my Facebook feed. Soon enough I notice that their conversation is actually an interview of some sort, and the man being interviewed seems strikingly intelligent. His answers are surprisingly nuanced and complex. I decide to look up and steal a glance at his name badge.

John Robison, it read.

It is none other than the John Elder Robison who authored *Look Me in the Eye*. I put down my phone and listen intently. When the interview hits a lull, I decide to introduce myself.

Nice to meet you, Elliot, says John. *What do you do? Are you a self-advocate?*

I didn't expect this question. How does he know? *Yes, but I'm also a researcher*, I say. *I work with Max Pinball at State University.*

John Elder Robison seems quite pleased with this answer. *Perfect! I was just talking about autistic autism researchers and wondering who to call. But here you are!* He speaks to the interviewer again. *Yes, there are many young people like Elliot here. And his mentor, Max Pinball, is truly excellent, fantastic. He is exactly the type of person who we should be funding.*

The interviewer nods at me and say[s...] interviewing John for an HBO show. He jots dow[n...] of notes. Unfortunately, I have a meeting scheduled i[n...] minutes. But as I stand and say goodbye, John also sta[nds.]

By the way, I say, *I'm also writing a memoir, partially in[spired by] inspiration from you. So thank you for writing books.*

John chuckles. He has probably heard this type of thing many times, but still, he says, *You're welcome.*

Later that day, I meet Dr. Pinball at a poster session. The poster hall is crowded, but he is easy to find due to being an outlier in height. (I have heard that he is 6'4", though I believe this may be an underestimation.) He excitedly waves me over and takes me to look at one poster in particular. It is a longitudinal study of youth with autism and comorbid bipolar disorder.

Cool poster, I say to the presenting author.

The author of the poster, a young woman, looks at me and smiles. *Are you on the spectrum, too?*

I nod, a bit shocked. *How did you know?*

My aspie radar is better than an ADOS, she says with a laugh.

I point to the last line of her poster. *The outcome for ASD+BP youth is favorable*, I read aloud. *What an inspirational quote!*

She laughs again. I walk back over to where Dr. Pinball is conspicuously lurking a few feet away. *Thanks for showing me that poster*, I say. *It was interesting.*

Dr. Pinball smiles. *I thought you'd like it. Do you like IMFAR?*

Yes!

I thought you would! He pauses, and then says, *You definitely have a place in this world, Elliot.*

I look around the room, which is too warm, crowded with bodies, and noisy—not exactly my favorite combination *physical place. This metaphorical place. You*

...nd final night of IMFAR I decide to ... the pier at night. It is a rather lengthy ...ed when I arrive there. The bright lights of downtown Baltimore twinkle like stars in the rippling darkness of the water, highlighting its vast, deep blackness. I sit alone on a bench by the edge of the pier.

I love to sing in front of large bodies of water. JS once asked me what my favorite place in the whole world was, and I told her it was the right-most swing on the beach in my hometown, where I loved to go at night and sing while swinging on the swing.

It is easy to frame my character traits in terms of autistic symptomology, or something related to it: insistence on sameness and routine, inflexibility, repetition, perseveration, poor emotional regulation. I am somewhat of an expert on these symptoms, so it is not difficult to pick them out in myself. But I prefer to think of it in another way: I have a deep and true love of certain things, certain topics, and indeed, certain people.

To me, to love someone is to love singing to them more than I love singing to the sea. It is a pure kind of love.

But I still love singing to the sea. It is like sending a message in a bottle. As a child, I imagined that if you sung to the sea, perhaps someone would hear you on the other side of the world. It would be someone you've never met. Someone you would probably never meet in your whole life. You would never get to speak to that person again, but for one instant, you would be connected. I have always been a romantic, I suppose.

I don't know what the future holds, nor can anyone. I know that it is up to me to decide where I will go from here.

Nobody can tell me this, and there is no diagnostic test for determining one's true identity (not even an ADOS).

Elliot Gavin Keenan

A Parade of Ghosts

There are ghosts here. The darkness looms over me. A relic, the remains of a Kirkbride building abandoned long ago. Its skeleton is a black shape cut out of the steely sky, imposing itself onto the horizon like a great mountain, like the Adirondacks to the north. But it is not a natural structure. Its bones are man-made, elegantly and purposefully constructed into wings and wards. A frigid breeze blows through the grass that lingers in the building's foreboding shadow, winds whistling through empty halls. I am far now from the car, left on the side of a road past a fence decorated with *Do Not Enter* signs. I am far now from the world I know. I am in their world: a quiet world.

Twenty years ago, this place died. But how many people died within this place? Maybe everyone who walked these halls died a little bit, left a piece of themselves behind to be preserved by the cold of a world frozen in time.

I stop my approach as the shadow engulfs me. There is a small side building, half-demolished, its gutted innards strewn across the lawn. Bricks upon bricks lay there in a heap. I hold one in small white hands, trembling from the shock of cold; its weight drags me down, grounding me here, to the piece of history forgotten by most.

The question is, what sort of ghosts?

In the distance, from within the shadowy figure of the main building's massive exoskeleton, a rowdy teenager shrieks and then laughs. He has come here as a schoolyard dare, a test of courage and youth, a rite of passage.

I turn over the brick in my hand and reddish dust crumbles into my palm. This is the piece of history I've come for. An inheritance. I've walked the narrow corridors of old Kirkbride buildings; I see the sky without walls now.

I look into the gray night. A stream of soft light flows from the moon, illuminating the pile of bricks before me. *Can I take this?* I say. I wait. A chilling gust ruffles my hair. There are ghosts here. People lived and died in these long halls. Are they the stuff of cheap horror films? Or are they as misunderstood in death as they were in life? These people never got to see the sky without walls. Not the parts of themselves they left behind, surrendered to time, to history. I take their silence as an affirmation. I take the brick with me on my journey back to the car, back to the real world, a place of motion and warmth and static and harsh blue light from phones and televisions. Away from this cold and gentle darkness. It invites me to stay under its calmly watchful eye, free now of clipboards and little plastic cups.

But the ritual I have come to complete is finished. There are ghosts here. This is their home, the only place they know. A year from now these halls will no longer exist. Long since forgotten by the general public. A history we would rather erase.

Come with me, I think; *follow me home*. I do not fear a parade of ghosts. I know what it is like to die alive.

Afterword

The gown is red, a sort of bright red like a robin's feathers, and it has a black stole draped over the shoulders with rainbow stripes at either end (quite explicitly an LGBT pride symbol); it hangs in wait on the back of my bedroom door.

I'm graduating in a month. And I've accepted a position as a doctoral student in a psychology program at UCLA. I talk to Dr. Pinball about it over bubble tea. He adjusts his spectacles and says, *I think the biggest challenge will be to reconcile your identity as an artist with your future as a scientist.* And he is right about this.

Where to begin?

I'm walking past Academy Street in my suburban hometown, a tiny hamlet on the bay, which once seemed to me a sprawling mess of flickering streetlamps and neatly trimmed front lawns. It's late at night, but I enjoy night walks. The air still smells of rain. Now that I've got a cigarette dangling from my mouth, I feel much more levelheaded than I did an hour ago (when I was crying on my bedroom floor).

In some ways, not much has changed; my thoughts are speeding by, just as they were at this time last year. *The trick*, says Dr. Pinball, *is to know how to deal with it*. That's something I'm still learning how to do. But I'm getting better. Writing has helped me, I think.

I pull the microphone down to my height and glance over the crowd. The little bakery-cafe is packed with poets of all skill levels. I suppose I am the youngest. They're looking at me expectantly. I pick a few smiling faces out of the audience: my boyfriend, and JS. And then I speak.

I see the audience react: curiosity, at first, and then bewilderment. Before I know it, I'm being greeted with applause, cheering, people calling me over who want to share with me their own stories, Susan Dingle who wants me to feature in July, my boyfriend who wants to kiss me, and JS, who is still smiling.

To my surprise, I find that I still know JS; which is to say, she knows the same jokes that she knew before, and has the same laugh. This is comforting to me.

I didn't forget her face. One day, I pick it out of a crowd and I wave to her, an awkward wave with a half-smile. And she stops, and smiles. At first I think I'm dreaming this, but I'm not. We sit on a bench in front of the psychology building and we do something we haven't done in a year: talk.

Dr. Pinball walks by. Later, he says, *She looked happy*. I nod. And he adds, *You looked happy, too*. And I was.

I find out that JS, too, has gotten involved with the creative writing department; that we've known many of the same people, in parallel.

I've been rooting for you, she says. And so was I.

I've spent my whole life looking for the people who would understand me. Sometimes I believed that they must be out there, somewhere, waiting for me. And I was right about this.

In some way, they've been there for me all along.

Sincerely yours,
Elliot

Elliot Gavin Keenan

Appendix A. Reputable Sources for More Information

National Alliance on Mental Illness (NAMI)
http://www.nami.org/

Autism Science Foundation (ASF)
http://autismsciencefoundation.org/

About the Author

Elliot Gavin Keenan is 21 years old and now a PhD student in Human Development & Psychology at UCLA. He has published a lyric essay in the literary journal Gravel. He has Asperger's syndrome and bipolar disorder. His research, which has been funded by the Autism Science Foundation, focuses on comorbidity in autism spectrum disorder. In his spare time he enjoys strategy board games, swing sets, and using italics.

Made in the USA
Middletown, DE
05 December 2017